CHENG & TSUI
"Bringing Asia to the World"™

中文听说读写 · 中文聽說讀寫

INTEGRATED CHINESE

Simplified and Traditional Characters

1

Character Workbook

4th Edition

Yuehua Liu and Tao-chung Yao
Nyan-Ping Bi, Liangyan Ge, Yaohua Shi

Original Edition by Tao-chung Yao and Yuehua Liu
Liangyan Ge, Yea-fen Chen, Nyan-Ping Bi, Xiaojun Wang, Yaohua Shi

CHENG & TSUI

"Bringing Asia to the World"™

Fourth Edition 2017
Third Edition 2009
Second Edition 2005
First Edition 1997

27 26 25 24 23 22   3 4 5 6 7

ISBN: 978-1-62291-137-0 [Fourth Edition]

Printed in the United States of America

The *Integrated Chinese* series includes textbooks, workbooks, character workbooks, teacher's resources, streaming audio, video, and more. Visit chengtsui.com for more information on the other components of *Integrated Chinese*.

Publisher
JILL CHENG

Editorial Manager
BEN SHRAGGE

Editor
LEI WANG

Creative Director
CHRISTIAN SABOGAL

Interior Design
KATE PAPADAKI

Cheng & Tsui Company, Inc.
Phone (617) 988-2400 / (800) 544-1963
Fax (617) 426-3669
25 West Street
Boston, MA 02111-1213 USA
chengtsui.com

CONTENTS

Preface

This completely revised and redesigned Character Workbook is meant to accompany the Fourth Edition of *Integrated Chinese* (IC). It has been about twenty years since the IC series came into existence in 1997. During these years, amid all the historical changes that took place in China and the rest of the world, the demand for Chinese language teaching/learning materials has grown dramatically. We are greatly encouraged by the fact that IC not only has been a widely used textbook at the college level all over the United States and beyond, but also has become increasingly popular for advanced language students in high schools. Based on user feedback, we have made numerous changes so that the Character Workbook can become an even more useful tool for students of Chinese.

Stressing the importance of learning a new character by its components

Learning a new character becomes much easier if the student can identify its components. The student should learn how to write the forty radicals at the beginning of the Character Workbook in the correct stroke order first, because these forty radicals will appear repeatedly in other characters later. If a new character contains a component already familiar to the student, the stroke order of that component will not be introduced again. However, we will show the stroke order of all new components as they appear when we introduce new characters. For example, when we introduce the character 孩 *(hái)* (child) in Lesson 2, we do not show the stroke order for the radical 子 *(zǐ)* (child) because 子 already appeared in the radical section. Therefore, we only display the stroke order for the other component 亥 *(hài)* (the last of the Twelve Earthly Branches). For the same reason, when 亥 appears in the new character 刻 *(kè)* (quarter of an hour) in Lesson 3, its stroke order is not displayed. When the student learns a new character, he or she can easily tell if a component in the character has appeared in previous lessons. If the stroke order for that component is not displayed, it means that the component is not new. The student should try to recall where he or she has seen it before. By doing so, the student can connect new characters with old ones and build up a character bank. We believe that learning by association will help the student memorize characters more effectively.

Main features of the new Character Workbook

a. Both traditional and simplified characters are introduced
If a character appears in both traditional and simplified form, we show both to accommodate different learner needs. Traditional characters are shown first.

b. Pinyin and English definition are clearly noted
We have moved the *pinyin* and the English definition above each character for easy recognition and review.

c. Radicals are highlighted
The radical of each character is highlighted. Knowing what radical group a character belongs to is essential when looking up that character in a traditional dictionary in which the characters are arranged according to their radicals. To a certain extent, radicals can also help the student decipher the meaning of a character. For example, characters containing the radical 貝／贝 *(bèi)* (shell), such as 貴／贵 *(guì)* (expensive), and 貨／货 *(huò)* (merchandise), are often associated with money or value. The student can group the characters sharing the same radical together and learn them by association.

d. Stroke order is prominently displayed

Another important feature is the numbering of each stroke in the order of its appearance. Each number is marked at the beginning of that particular stroke. We firmly believe that it is essential to write a character in the correct stroke order, and to know where each stroke begins and ends. To display the stroke order more prominently, we have moved the step-by-step character writing demonstration next to the main characters.

e. "Training wheels" are provided

We also provide grids with fine shaded lines inside to help the student better envision and balance their characters when practicing.

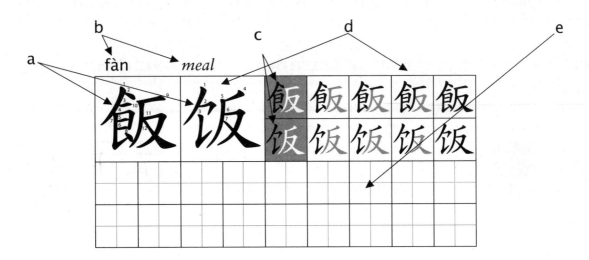

Other changes

In response to user feedback, we have updated the traditional characters to ensure they match the standard set currently used in Taiwan. For reference, we have consulted the Taiwan Ministry of Education's *Revised Chinese Dictionary*. This change has been overseen by the editors.

In order to focus on character recognition and acquisition, we decided not to include elements having to do with phonetic identification and phrase recognition.

To help the student look up characters more easily, we decided to limit the indices to two: one arranged alphabetically by *pinyin* and the other by lesson. Additional appendices that are not directly linked to the practice of writing characters, such as the English-Chinese glossary, are available in the Textbook.

The formation of the radicals in this book are based on the *Modern Chinese Dictionary* (現代漢語詞典/現代汉语词典) published by the Commercial Press (商務印書館/商务印书馆). A total of 201 radicals appear in that dictionary, and in some cases the same character is listed under more than one radical. For the characters in this book that fall in that category, we provide two radicals in order to facilitate students' dictionary searches. The two radicals are presented in order from top to bottom (e.g., 名：夕，口), left to right (e.g., 功：工，力), and large to small (e.g., 章：音，立；麻：麻，广).

The changes that we made in the new version reflect the collective wishes of the users. We would like to take this opportunity to thank those who gave us feedback on how to improve the Character Workbook. We would like to acknowledge in particular Professor Hu Shuangbao of Peking University and Professor Shi Dingguo of Beijing Language and Culture University, both of whom read the entire manuscript and offered invaluable comments and suggestions for revision.

Note: Prefaces to the previous editions of IC are available at chengtsui.co.

Basics

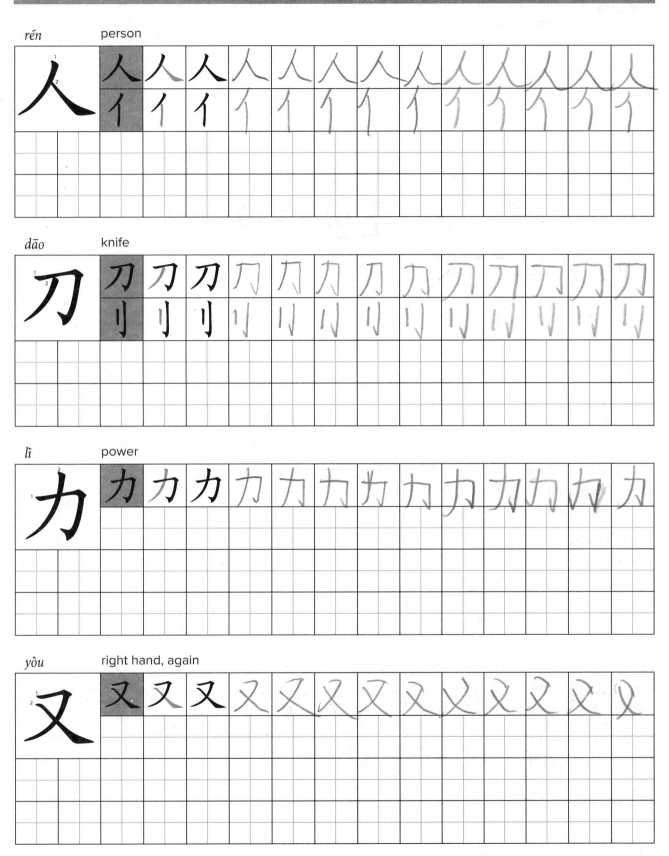

rén — person

dāo — knife

lì — power

yòu — right hand, again

kǒu   mouth

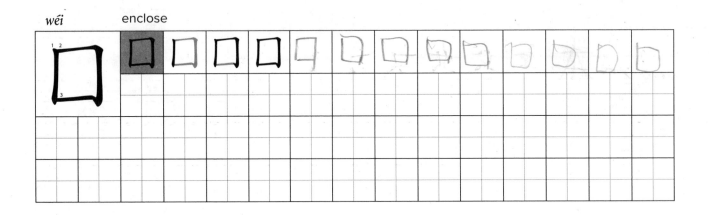

wéi   enclose

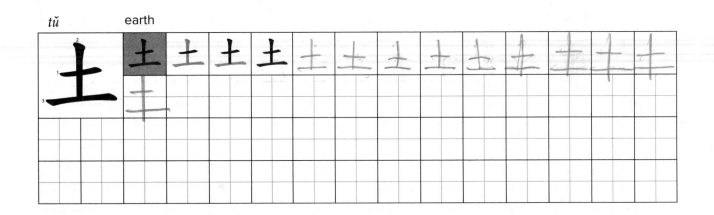

_tǔ_   earth

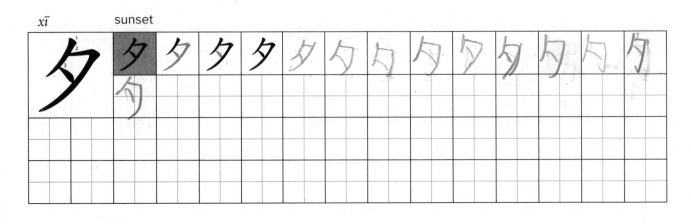

_xī_   sunset

dà　　big

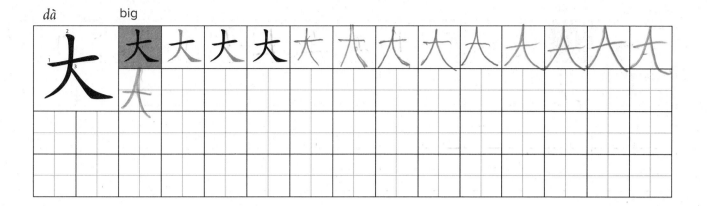

nǚ　　woman

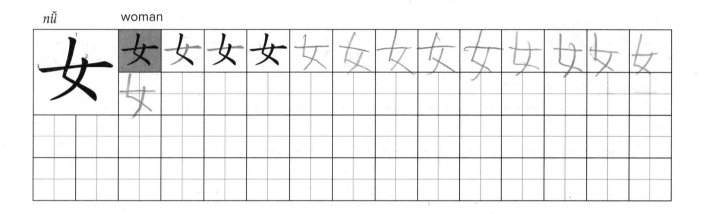

zǐ　　child

cùn　　inch

xiǎo small

小 | 小 小 小 小 小 小 小 小 小 小 小 小 小

gōng labor, work

工 | 工 工 工 工 工 工 工 工 工 工 工 工

yāo tiny, small

幺 | 幺 幺 幺 幺 幺 幺 幺 幺 幺 幺 幺 幺

gōng bow

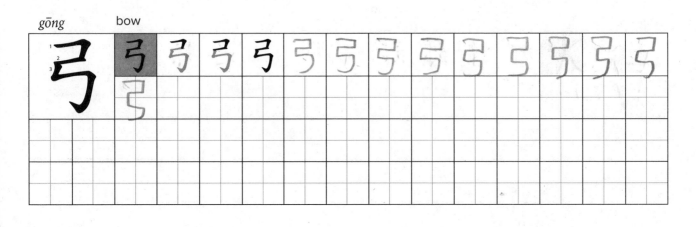

弓 | 弓 弓 弓 弓 弓 弓 弓 弓 弓 弓 弓 弓 弓

xīn   heart

心 心 心 心 心 心 心 心 心 心 心 心 心 心
忄 忄 忄 忄 忄 忄 忄 忄 忄 忄 忄 忄 忄 忄

心 心
忄

gē   dagger-axe

戈 戈 戈 戈 戈 戈 戈 戈 戈 戈 戈 戈 戈 戈
戈 戈

shǒu   hand

手 手 手 手 手 手 手 手 手 手 手 手 手 手
扌 扌 扌 扌 扌 扌 扌 扌 扌 扌 扌 扌 扌 扌

手 手
扌 扌

rì   sun

日 日 日 日 日 日 日 日 日 日 日 日 日 日
日 日

yuè moon

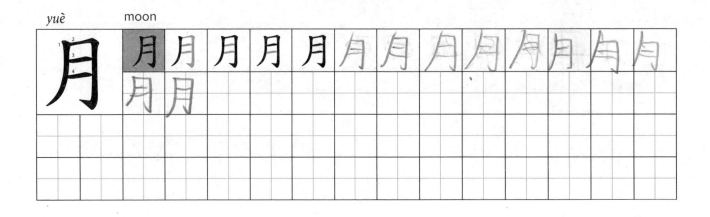

_mù_ wood

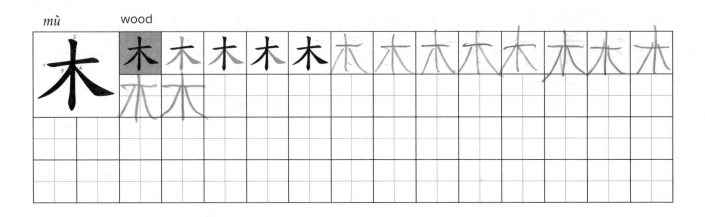

shuǐ water

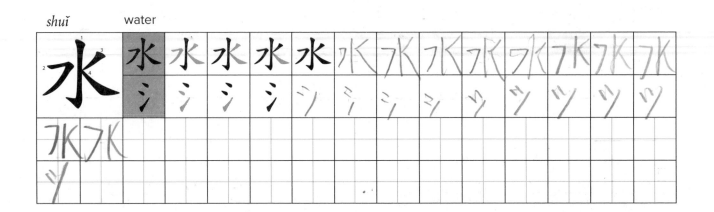

huǒ fire

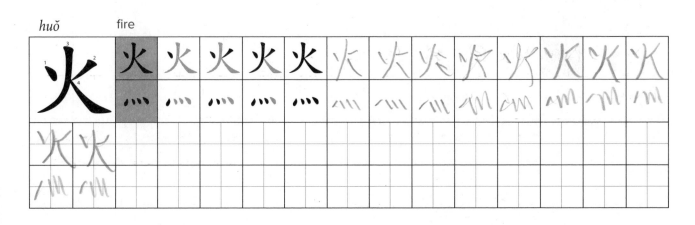

tián   field

田

mù   eye

目

shì   show

示

mì   fine silk

糸

ěr ear

耳

yī clothing

衣
衤

yán speech

言
讠

bèi cowrie shell

貝 贝

zǒu　　walk

走　走 走 走 走 走 走 走 走 走 走 走 走 走

zú　　foot

足　足 足 足 足 足 足 足 足 足 足 足 足 足
　　　足 足 足 足 足 足 足 足 足 足 足 足 足

jīn　　gold

金　金 金 金 金 金 金 金 金
　　金 金 金 金 金 金 金 金
　　钅 钅 钅 钅 钅 钅

金 金 金 金 金
金 金 金 金 金
钅 钅 钅 钅 钅

mén　　door

門 门　門 門 門 門 門 門 門 門
　　　门 门 门 门

門 門 門 門 門
门 门 门 门 门

zhuī   short-tailed bird

隹 佳 佳 佳 佳 佳 佳 佳 佳

yǔ   rain

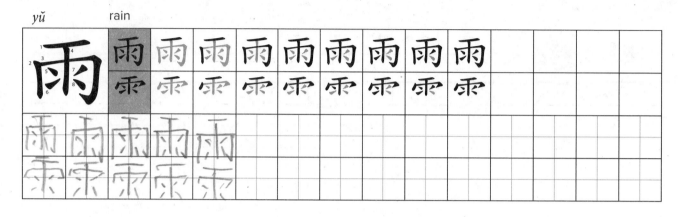

雨

shí   eat

食

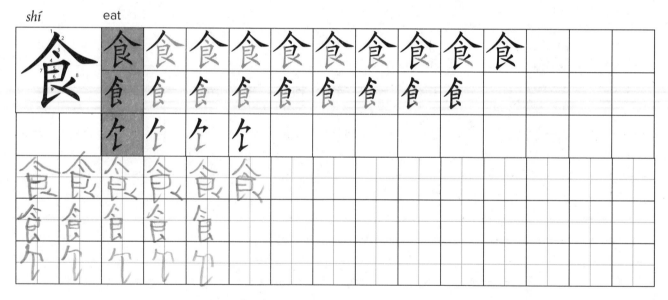

mǎ   horse

馬 马

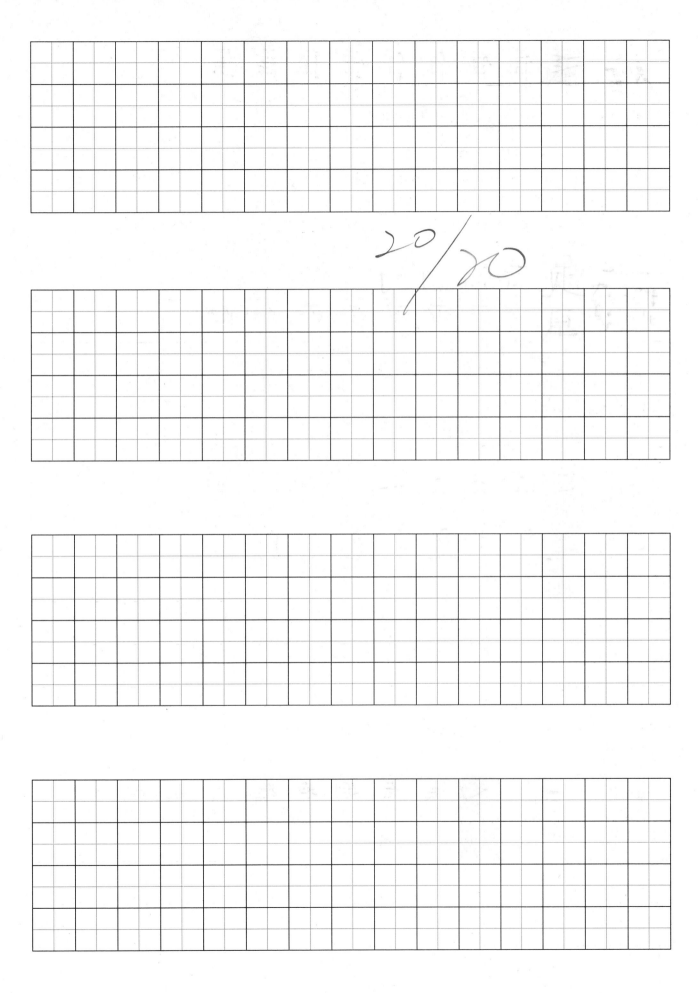

20/20

Basics

yī   one

èr   two

sān   three

sì   four

wǔ five

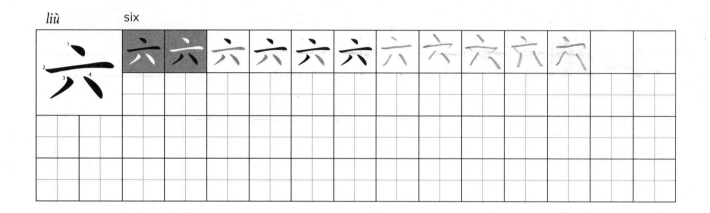

liù six

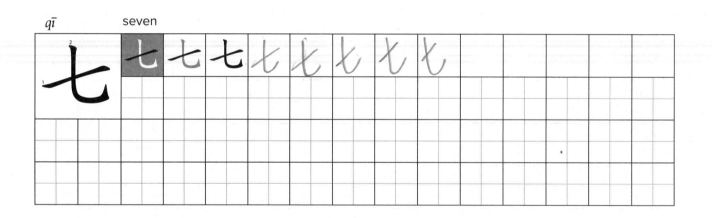

qī seven

七七七七七七七七

bā eight

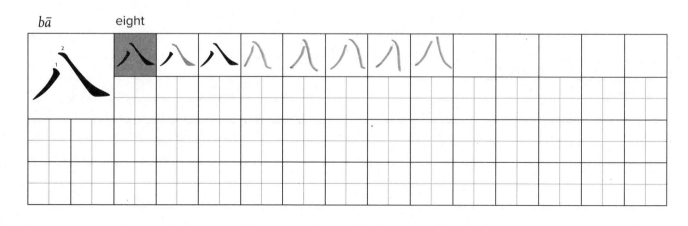

jiŭ nine

九 九 九 九 九 九 九 九 九 九

shí ten

十 十 十 十 十 十 十 十 十

Lesson 1: Greetings

Dialogue 1: Exchanging Greetings

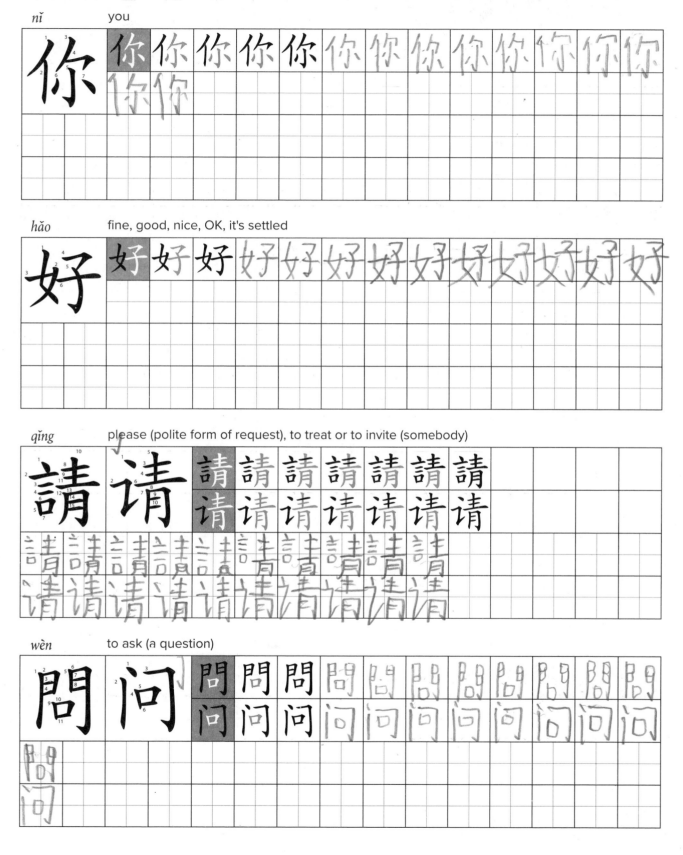

nǐ — you

hǎo — fine, good, nice, OK, it's settled

qǐng — please (polite form of request), to treat or to invite (somebody)

wèn — to ask (a question)

guì   honorable, expensive

貴   贵

xìng   (one's) family name is . . . ; famiy name

姓

wǒ   I, me

我

ne   (question particle)

呢

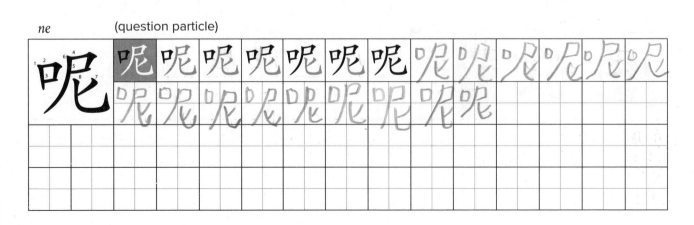

jiě older sister

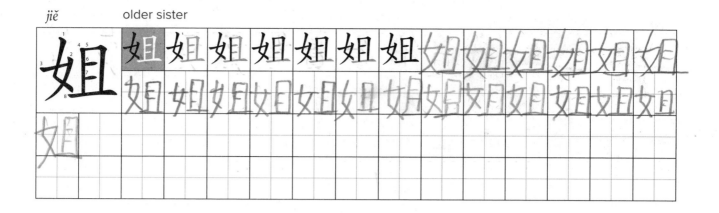

jiào to be called, to call

shén what

me (question particle)

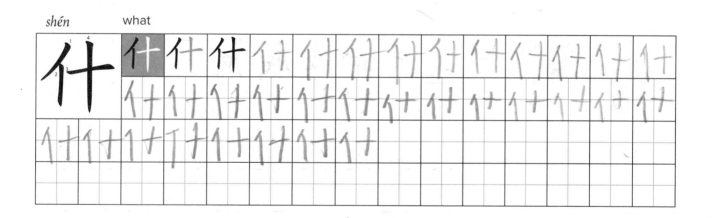

míng name

名

名 名 名 名 名 名 名 名 名 名 名 名 名

zì character

字

字 字 字 字 字 字 字 字 字

xiān first

先

先 先 先 先 先 先 先 先 先 先 先 先

shēng to give birth to, to be born

生

生 生 生 生 生 生 生 生 生 生 生

Characters from Proper Nouns

lǐ   (a family name), plum

yǒu   friend

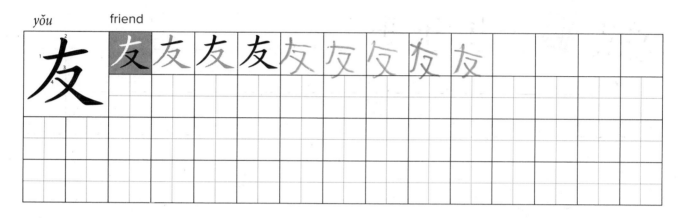

wáng   (a family name), king

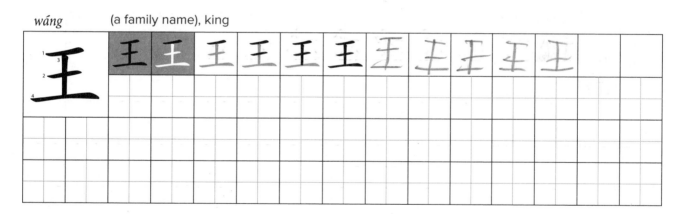

péng   friend

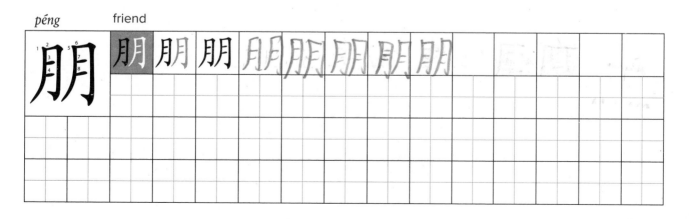

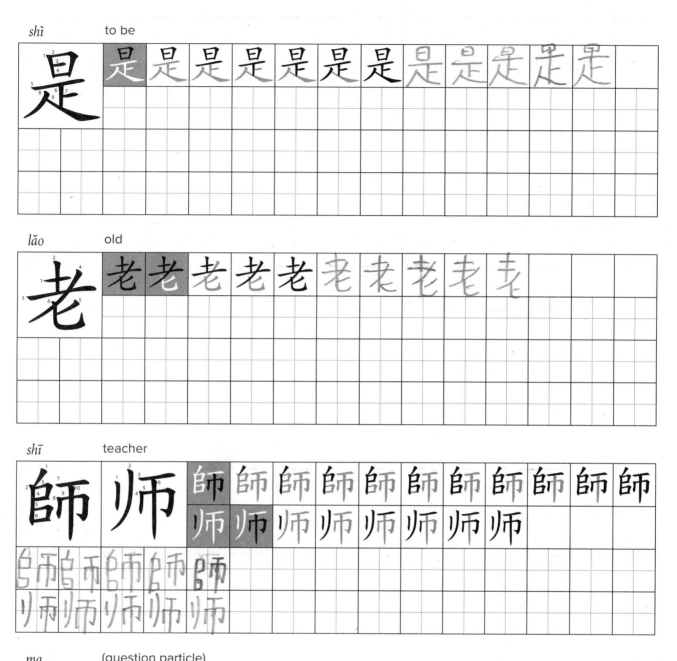

shì   to be

是

lǎo   old

老

shī   teacher

師 师

ma   (question particle)

嗎 吗

bù not, no

不 不 不 不 不 不 不 不 不 不

xué to study

學 學 學 學 學 學 學 學 學 學 學
學 學 學 學 學 學 學 學 學
学 学 学 学 学 学 学

学 学 学 学 学

yě too, also

也 也 也 也 也 也 也 也 也 也

rén people, person

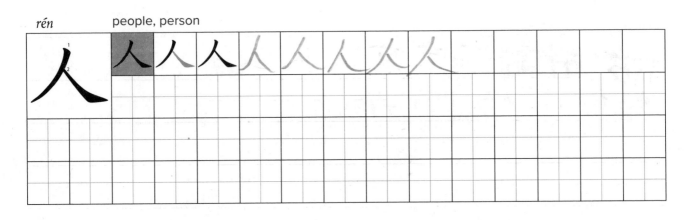

人 人 人 人 人 人 人 人

Characters from Proper Nouns

zhōng   center, middle

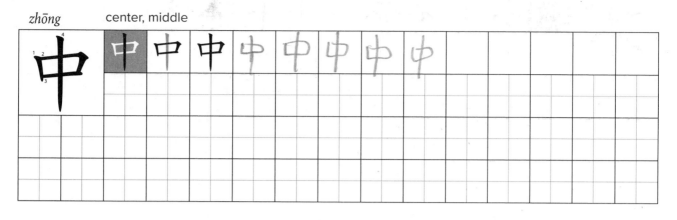

guó   country, nation

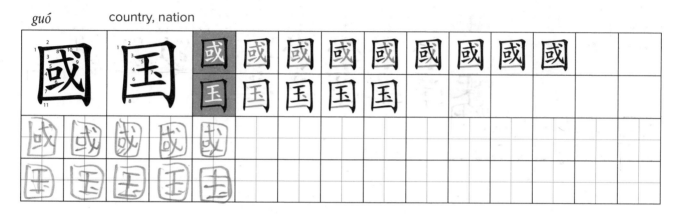

běi   north

jīng   capital city

měi   beautiful

美 美 美 美 美 美 美 美 美

美 美 美 美 美 美 美 美 美 美

niǔ   knob, button

紐 纽 紐 紐 紐 紐 紐 紐 紐 紐 紐 紐
            纽 纽 纽 纽 纽 纽 纽 纽 纽 纽 纽

yuē   agreement, appointment

約 约 約 約 約 約 約 約 約 約 約 約 約
            约 约 约 约 约 约 约 约 约 约

10/10

Lesson 2: Family

Dialogue 1: Looking at a Family Photo

zhè (partial, cut off in corner)

*nà**   that

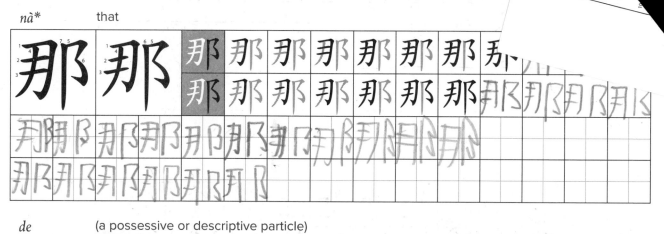

de   (a possessive or descriptive particle)

zhào   photograph; to illuminate, to shine

照

piàn   flat, thin piece

片

* Some simplified and traditional characters that appear identical are technically considered to have a different number of strokes. Where this is the case, we present the stroke orders for both the simplified and traditional versions of the character to highlight this difference.

this

這 这 | 这 这 这 这 这 | 这 这 这 这 这 这
这 | 这 这 这 这 这 | 这 这 这 这 这 这

bà   father, dad

爸 | 爸 爸 爸 爸 爸 爸 爸 爸 爸

mā   mother, mom

媽 妈 | 媽 媽 媽 媽 媽 媽 媽 媽 媽 媽
妈 | 妈 妈 妈 妈 妈 妈 妈 妈 妈 妈

gè/ge   (measure word for many common everyday objects)

個 个 | 個 個 個 個 個 個 個 個 個 個
个 | 个 个 个 个 个 个 个 个 个

hái   child

孩   孩 孩 孩 孩 孩 孩 孩 孩 孩 孩 孩 孩 孩

孩 孩 孩 孩 孩

shéi   who

誰 谁   誰 誰 誰 誰 誰 誰 誰 誰 誰 誰 誰
        谁 谁 谁 谁 谁 谁 谁 谁 谁 谁 谁

誰 誰 誰 誰
谁 谁 谁 谁

tā   she, her

她   她 她 她 她 她 她 她 她 她 她 她 她

nán   male

男   男 男 男 男 男 男 男 男 男 男 男 男
      男 男

dì — younger brother

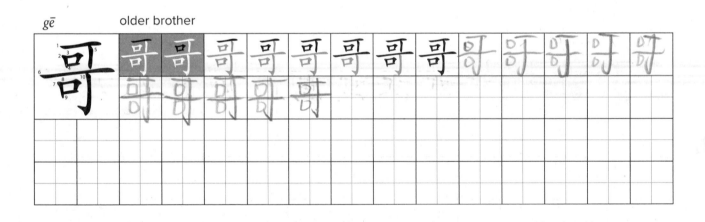

弟

tā — he, him

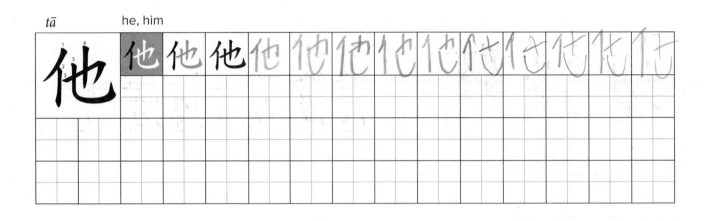

他

gē — older brother

哥

ér — son, child

兒 儿

yǒu   to have, to exist

有

méi   not

沒

Characters from Proper Nouns

gāo   (a family name), tall, high

高

wén   (written) language, script

文

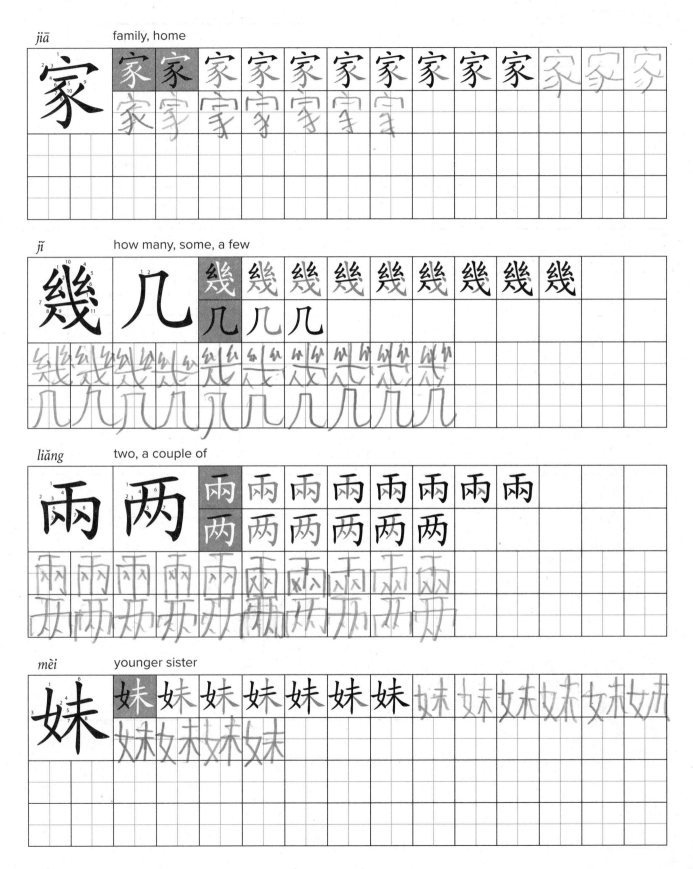

jiā   family, home

jǐ   how many, some, a few

liǎng   two, a couple of

mèi   younger sister

hé   and

和

zuò   to do

做

zuò   to work, to do

作

lǜ   law, rule

律

dōu   both, all

都 都

yī   doctor, medicine

醫 医

Characters from Proper Nouns

bái   (a family name), white

白

yīng   flower, hero, Britain

英 英

ài   love; to love

I'm not sure why you lessons 3-4 are already done.

If it's not done by you. You should write your own character practices

Talk to me about this.   10/60

Lesson 3: Time and Date

Dialogue 1: Out for a Birthday Dinner

hào (measure word for position in a numeral series, day of the month)

號 号 | 號 號 號 號 號 號 號 號 號 號
号 | 号 号 号 号 号 号 号 号

xīng star

星 | 星 星 星 星 星 星 星 星 星 星 星 星

qī period (of time)

期 | 期 期 期 期 期 期 期 期 期 期 期 期

tiān day

天 | 天 天 天 天 天 天 天 天 天 天 天 天

jīn — today, now

今

nián — year

年

年 年 年 年 年 年 年 年 年 年 年 年
年 年 年 年

duō — how many/much, to what extent

多

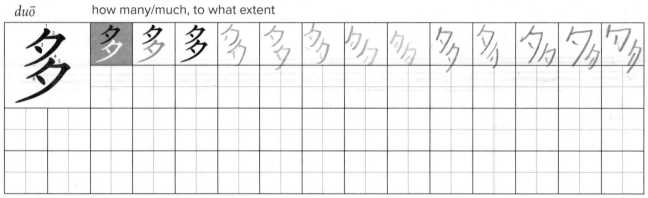

suì — year (of age)

歲 岁

歲 歲 歲 歲 歲 歲 歲 歲 歲 歲
歲 歲 歲 歲 歲 歲 歲 歲 歲
岁 岁 岁 岁 岁 岁 岁 岁 岁 岁

歲 歲 歲
岁 岁 岁 岁

chī   to eat

fàn   meal, (cooked) rice

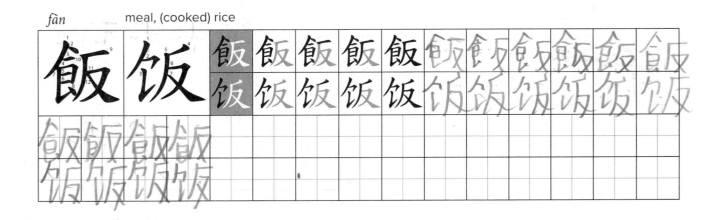

zěn   how

怎

yàng   shape, appearance, manner

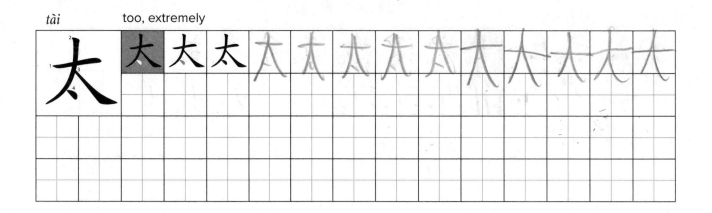

tài   too, extremely

太

le   (particle)

了

xiè   to thank

謝 谢

xǐ   to like; happy

喜

huān	happy, joyous										

歡 欢

cài	dish, cuisine										

菜 菜

hái	still, additionally, alternatively										

還 还

kě	but										

可

們 们 們 們 們 們 們 們 們 們 們 們

diǎn   o'clock (lit. dot, point, thus "points on the clock")

Traditional / simplified

點 点 點 點 點 點 點 點 點 點 點 點

bàn   half, half an hour

半 半 半 半 半 半 半 半 半 半 半 半

wǎn   evening, late

晚 晚 晚 晚 晚 晚 晚 晚 晚 晚 晚 晚

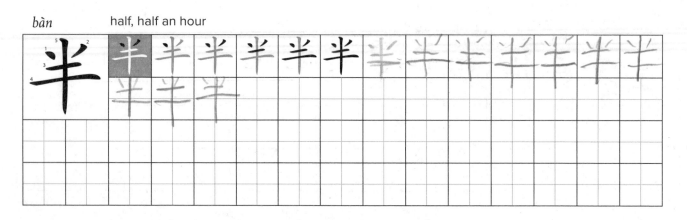

shàng above; top

上 上 上 上 上 上 上 上 上 上 上 上 上

jiàn to see

見 见 見 見 見 見 見 見 見 見 見 見
见 见 见 见 见 见 见 见 见
見 見 見

zài again

再 再 再 再 再 再 再 再 再 再 再 再 再
再 再 再 再 再

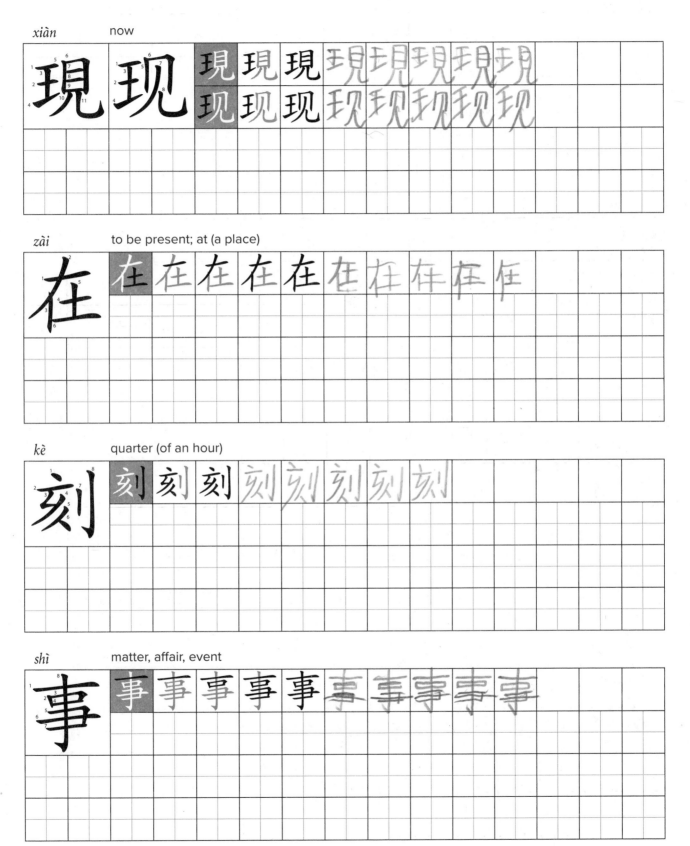

xiàn   now

zài   to be present; at (a place)

kè   quarter (of an hour)

shì   matter, affair, event

hěn   very

很

máng   busy

忙

míng   bright

明

wèi   for

為   为

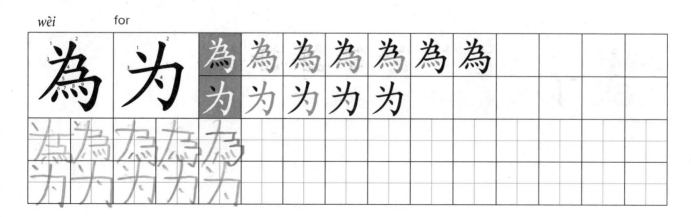

yīn   cause, reason; because

因　因 因 因 因 因　因 因 因 因 因

tóng   same

同　同 同 同 同 同　同 同 同 同

rèn   to recognize

認 认　認 認 認 認 認　認 認 認 認 認
　　认　认 认 认 认 认　认 认 认 认 认

7.5/10   You can resubmit.

shí   to recognize

識 识　識 識 識 識 識 識 識　識 識 識 識
　　识　识 识 识 识 识 识 识　识 识 识 识

識
识

① D2 needs another 5 times for
each character.
② only write simplied character now (p.42)

Lesson 4: Hobbies

Dialogue 1: Discussing Hobbies

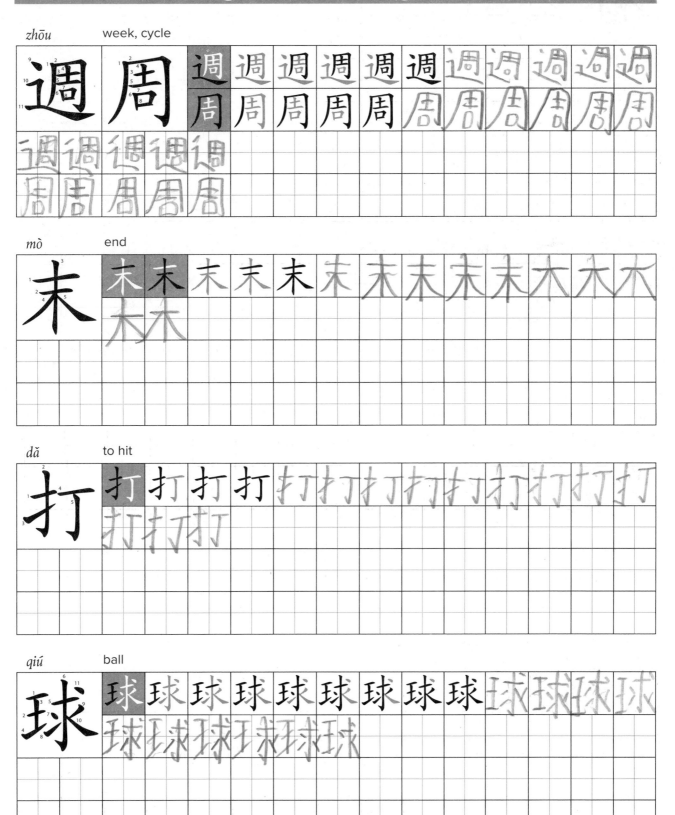

zhōu   week, cycle

mò   end

dǎ   to hit

qiú   ball

kàn to watch, to look, to read

看 看 看 看 看 看 看 看 看 看 看 看 看 看

diàn electricity

電 电 電 電 電 電 電 電 電 電 電
電 电 电 电 电 电 电 电 电 电

shì vision

視 视 視 視 視 視 視 視 視 視 視 視 視
視 视 視 視 視 視 視 視 視 視 視 視

視 視 視
視 視 視

chàng to sing

唱 唱 唱 唱 唱 唱 唱 唱 唱 唱 唱 唱 唱
唱

gē song

歌 | 歌 | 歌 | 歌 | 歌歌歌歌歌歌歌歌歌歌

tiào to jump

跳 | 跳 | 跳 | 跳 | 跳 | 跳 | 跳 | 跳 | 跳跳跳跳跳

wǔ to dance; dance

舞 | 舞 | 舞 | 舞 | 舞 | 舞 | 舞 | 舞 | 舞 | 舞 | 舞 | 舞
舞 舞舞舞舞舞舞

tīng to listen

聽听 | 聽 听 | 聽 听 | 聽 听 | 聽 听 | 聽 听 | 聽 听 | 聽听 聽听 聽听 聽听

yīn — sound

音

音 音 音 音 音 音 音 音 音 音 音 音

yuè — music

樂 乐

樂 樂 樂 樂 樂 樂 樂 樂 樂 樂 樂 樂
乐 乐 乐 乐 乐 乐 乐 乐 乐 乐 乐 乐

Traditional = Don't write this
↓

shū — book

書 书

書 書 書 書 書 書 書 書 書 書 書 書
书 书 书 书 书 书 书 书 书 书 书 书

↑
Simplied
Write this X 10 times

duì — right, correct

對 对

對 對 對 對 對 對 對 對 對 對
对 对 对 对 对 对 对 对 对 对

對 對 對

shí   time

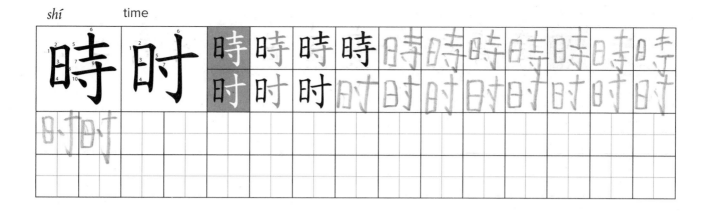

hòu   time, season; await

yǐng   shadow

cháng   often

qù   to go

去

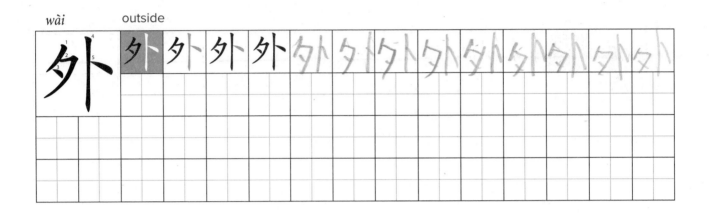

wài   outside

外

kè   guest

客

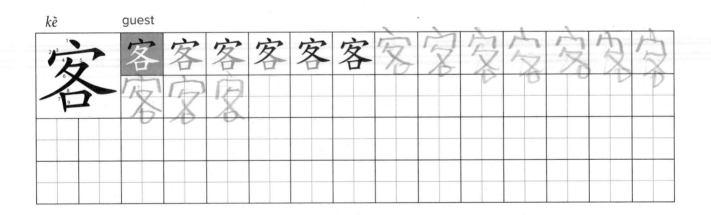

zuó   yesterday

昨

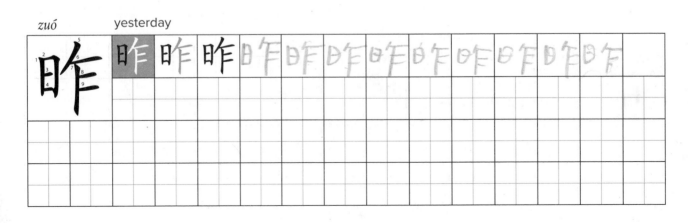

suǒ   place; (component of 所以: therefore, so)

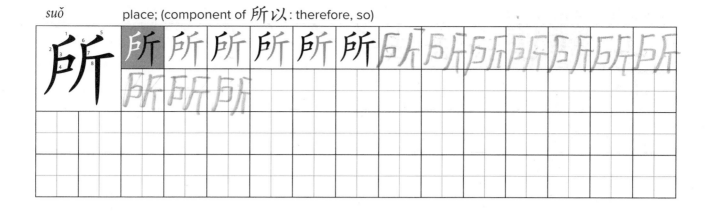

yǐ   with

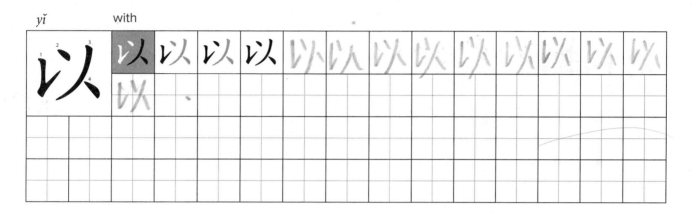

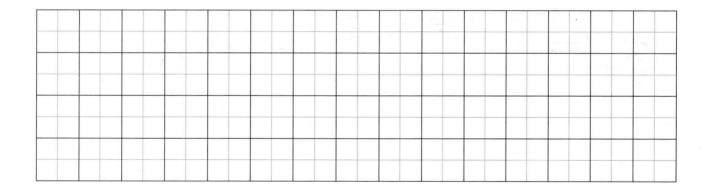

jiǔ long (of time)

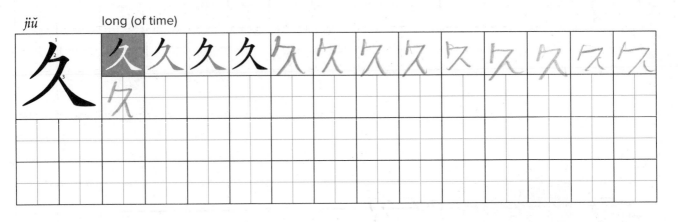

cuò wrong

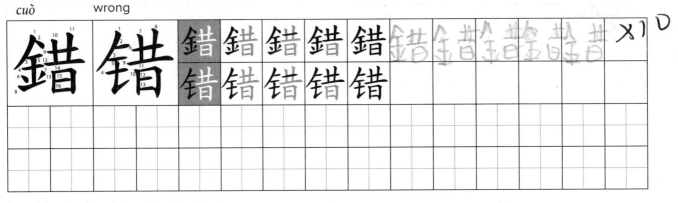

×10

xiǎng to want to, would like to

想 想 想 想

×10

jué to feel, to think

×10

de   (particle)

得　得 得 得 得 得 得 得 得 得 得　×10

yì   meaning

意　意 意 意 意 意 意 意 意 意 意 意

sī   to think

思　思 思 思 思 思 思 思 思 思 思 思 思
思

zhǐ   only

只　只 只 只 只 只 只 只 只 只 只 只 只
只

shuì to sleep

睡 睡 | 睡 睡 睡 睡 睡 睡 睡 睡 睡
睡 睡 睡 睡 睡 睡 睡 睡 睡

suàn to calculate

算 | 算 算 算 算 算 算 算 算 算
算 算 算 算 算 X10

zhǎo to look for

找 | 找 找 找 找 找 找 找 找 X10

bié other

別 別 | 別 別 別 別 別 別 別 別 別 別 X10
別 別 別 別

9/10 See my comment on P52

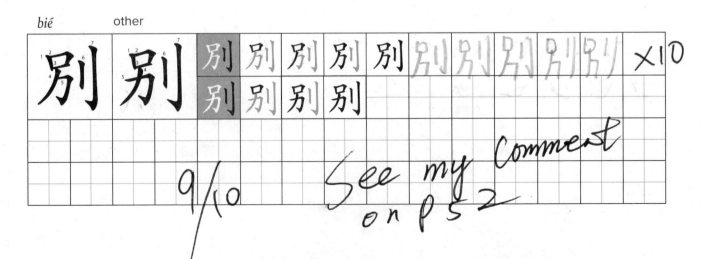

Lesson 5: Visiting Friends

Dialogue: Visiting a Friend's Place

ya   (interjectory particle used to soften a question)

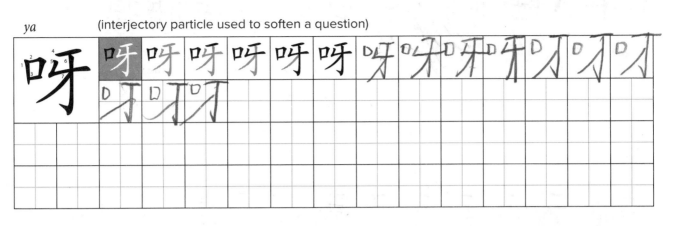

jìn   to enter

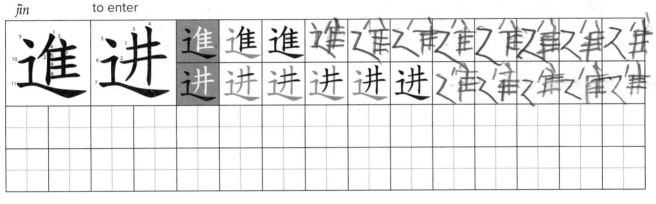

kuài   fast, quick; quickly

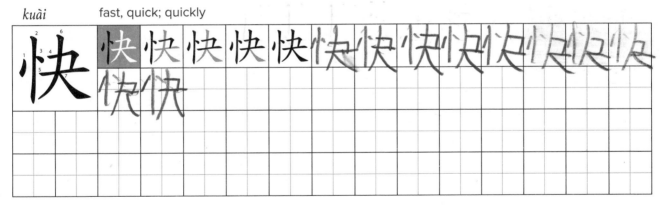

lái   to come

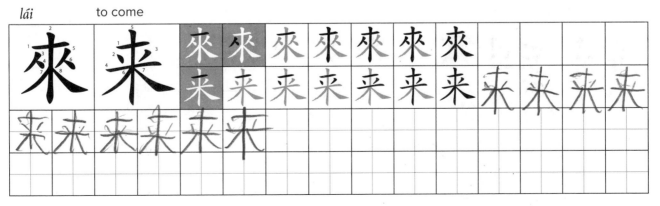

jiè   to be situated between

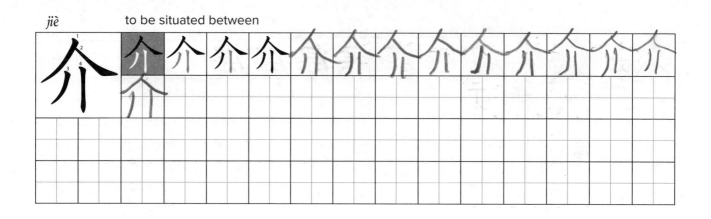

shào   to carry on, to continue

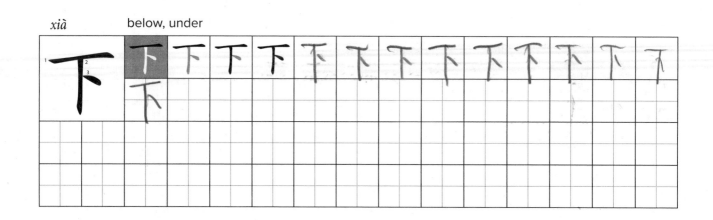

xià   below, under

xìng   mood, interest

piào (component of 漂亮: pretty)

漂

亮 亮

坐

哪 哪

liàng bright

zuò to sit

nǎ where

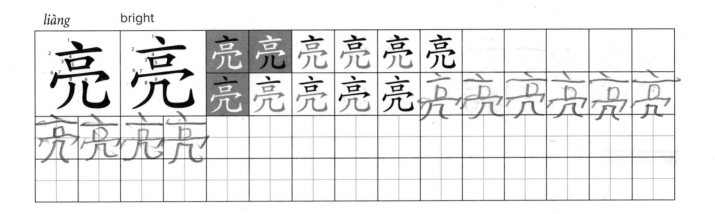

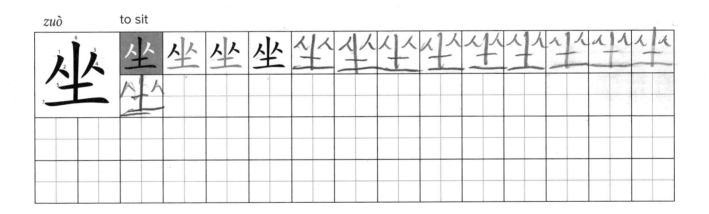

xiào   school

校 | 校 | 校 | 校 | 校

hē   to drink

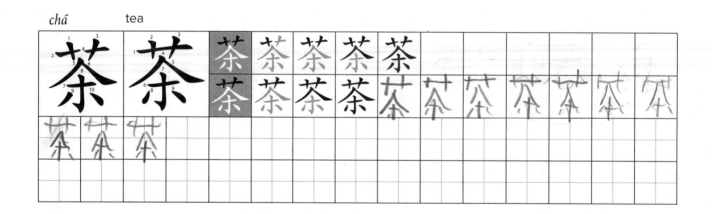

喝 | 喝 | 喝 | 喝 | 喝 | 喝 | 喝

chá   tea

茶 | 茶 | 茶 | 茶 | 茶 | 茶

kā   (component of 咖啡: coffee)

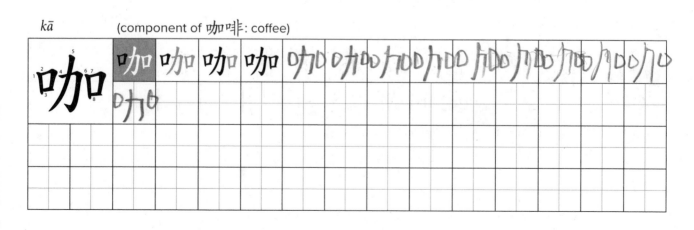

咖 | 咖 | 咖 | 咖

fēi (component of 咖啡: coffee)

啡 | 啡 | 啡 | 啡 | 啡 | 啡 | 啡 | 啡 | 啡 | 啡 | 啡 | 啡 | 啡
啡 | 啡 | 啡 | 啡 | 啡

ba (a sentence-final particle)

吧 | 吧 | 吧 | 吧 | 吧 | 吧 | 吧 | 吧 | 吧 | 吧 | 吧 | 吧 | 吧

yào to want

要 | 要 | 要 | 要 | 要 | 要 | 要 | 要 | 要 | 要 | 要
要

píng (measure word for bottled liquid)

瓶 | 瓶 | 瓶 | 瓶 | 瓶 | 瓶 | 瓶 | 瓶 | 瓶 | 瓶 | 瓶 | 瓶 | 瓶
瓶 | 瓶 | 瓶 | 瓶 | 瓶 | 瓶 | 瓶 | 瓶 | 瓶

qǐ   to rise

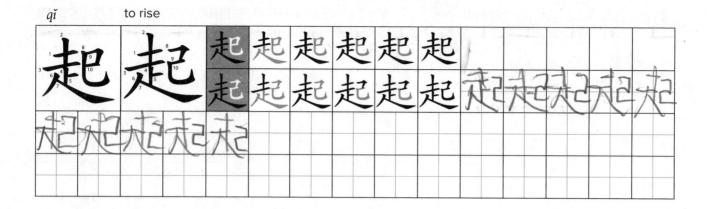

gěi   to give

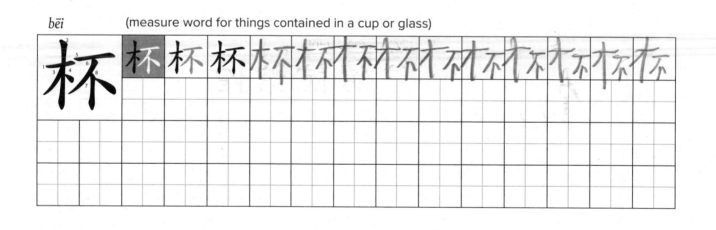

bēi   (measure word for things contained in a cup or glass)

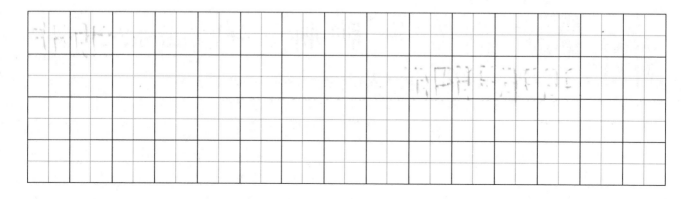

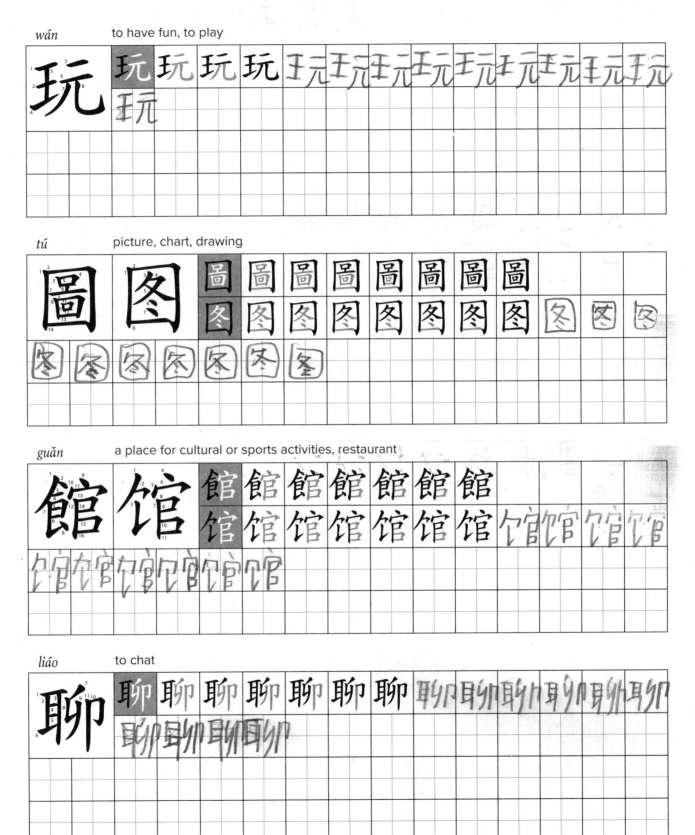

wán — to have fun, to play

玩

tú — picture, chart, drawing

圖 图

guǎn — a place for cultural or sports activities, restaurant

館 馆

liáo — to chat

聊

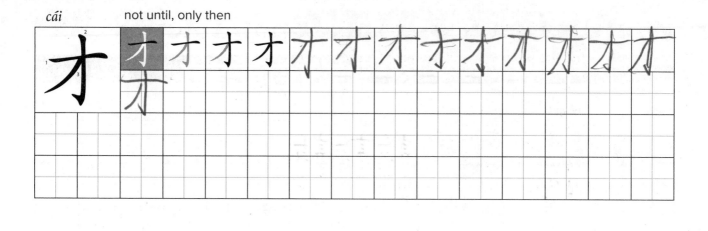

cái   not until, only then

才

huí   to return

回

Lesson 6: Making Appointments

Dialogue 1: Calling Your Teacher

huà　　speech

話　话　話 話 話 話 話
　　　　话 话 话 话 话

wéi/wèi　　(on telephone) Hello!, Hey!

喂　喂 喂 喂 喂 喂 喂

jiù　　precisely, exactly

就　就 就 就 就 就 就 就 就 就 就

nín　　you (honorific for 你)

您　您 您 您

wèi   (polite measure word for people)

位　位 位 位

wǔ   noon

午　午 午 午 午 午

jiān   during (a time period), between (two sides)

間 间　間 間 間
　　　　间 间 间

tí   topic, question

題 题　題 題 題 題 題 題
　　　題 题 题 题 题 题

kāi   to open, to hold (a meeting, party, etc.)

開 开 開 開 開
開 开 开 开 开

huì   meeting

會 会 會 會 會 會 會 會 會 會 會 會
會 会 会 会 会 会

jié   (measure word for class periods)

節 节 節 節 節 節 節 節 節
節 节 节 节 节 节

kè   class, course, lesson

課 课 課 課 課 課
課 课 课 课 课 课

jí　　level, rank

級 级 级级级级级级
　　　级级级级级

kǎo　　to give or take a test

考 考考考考考考

shì　　test; to try, to experiment

試 试 試試試試試試
　　　试试试试试试

hòu　　after, behind, rear

後 后 後後後後後
　　　后后后后后后

kòng free time

空

空 空 空 空 空

fāng square, method

方

方 方 方 方 方

biàn convenient, handy

便

便 便 便 便 便 便

dào to go to, to arrive

到

到 到 到 到 到 到 到

bàn   to manage

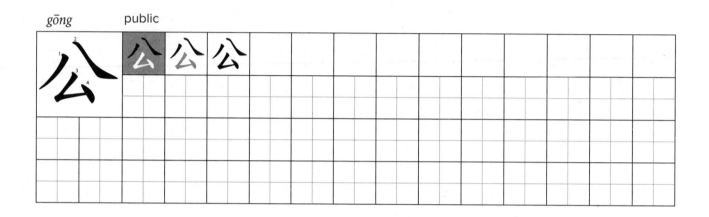

gōng   public

shì   room

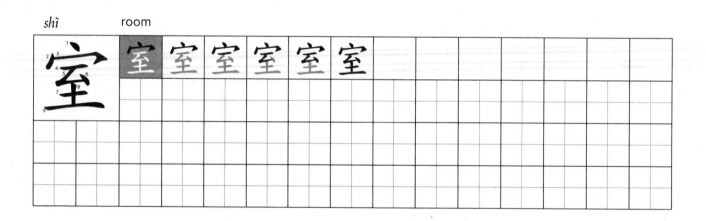

xíng   all right, OK

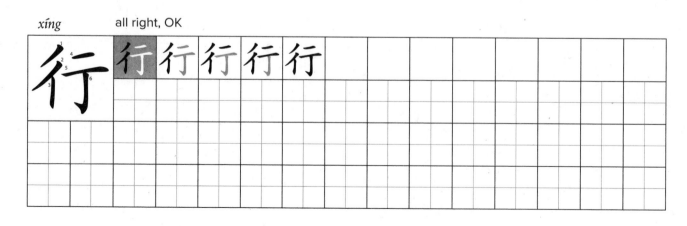

děng   to wait, to wait for

等 等 等 等

qì   air

氣 气 氣 氣 氣 氣 氣 氣 氣 氣 氣 氣 氣
气 气 气 气 气

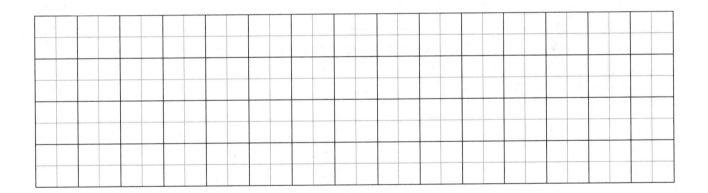

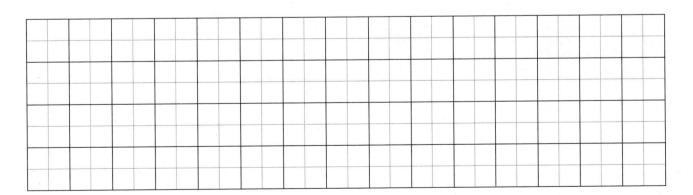

Dialogue 2: Calling a Friend for Help

bāng — to help

幫 帮 幫幫幫幫幫幫 帮帮帮帮帮

zhǔn — standard, criterion

準 准 準準準準準 准准准准

bèi — to prepare

備 备 備備備備備備備備 备备备备备备

liàn — to drill

練 练 練練練練練練練練 练练练练练练

xí   to practice

習 习 習 習 習 習 習 習 習
        习 习 习 习 习

shuō   to say, to speak

說 说 說 說 說 說 說 說
        说 说 说 说 说 说

a   (a sentence-final particle of exclamation, interrogation, etc.)

啊 啊 啊 啊 啊 啊 啊 啊
        啊 啊 啊 啊 啊

dàn   but

但 但 但 但 但

gēn　　with

跟　跟 跟 跟

miàn　　face

面　面 面 面 面 面 面 面 面 面 面

Lesson 7: Studying Chinese

Dialogue 1: How Did You Do on the Exam?

fù   to repeat, to duplicate

復 复 復 復 復 復 復
           复 复 复 复 复

xiě   to write

寫 写 寫 寫 寫 寫 寫
           写 写 写 写 写

màn   slow

慢 慢 慢 慢 慢 慢

zhī   (measure word for long, thin, inflexible objects such as pens, pencils, etc.)

枝 枝 枝 枝 枝

bǐ   pen

筆 笔 | 笔 笔 笔 笔 笔 笔 笔

zhāng   (measure word for flat objects such as paper, pictures, etc.)

張 张 | 張 張 張 張 張 張 張 張 張 张 張 张 张 张 张 张 张

zhǐ   paper

紙 纸 | 紙 紙 紙 紙 紙 紙 纸 纸 纸 纸 纸 纸

jiāo   to teach

教 | 教 教 教 教 教 教 教

dǒng   to understand

懂　懂　懂 懂 懂 懂 懂 懂 懂 懂 懂
　　　　懂 懂 懂 懂 懂 懂 懂 懂 懂

zhēn   true; real(ly)

真　真 真 真 真 真 真 真 真 真

lǐ   inside

裡　里　裡 裡 裡
　　　　里 里

yù   in advance; beforehand

預　预　預 預 預 預 預 預
　　　　预 预 预 预 预 预

dì (prefix for ordinal numbers)

第 第第第

yǔ language

語语 語語語語
语语语语

fǎ law, rule, method

法 法法法

róng to allow, to tolerate

容 容容容容容

yì   easy

易 | 日 易 易 易 易

cí   word

詞 词 | 詞 詞 詞 詞 詞 / 词 词 词 词 词

hàn   Chinese ethnicity

漢 汉 | 漢 漢 漢 / 汉 汉 汉

nán   difficult

難 难 | 難 難 難 難 難 難 難 難 難 / 难 难 难 难

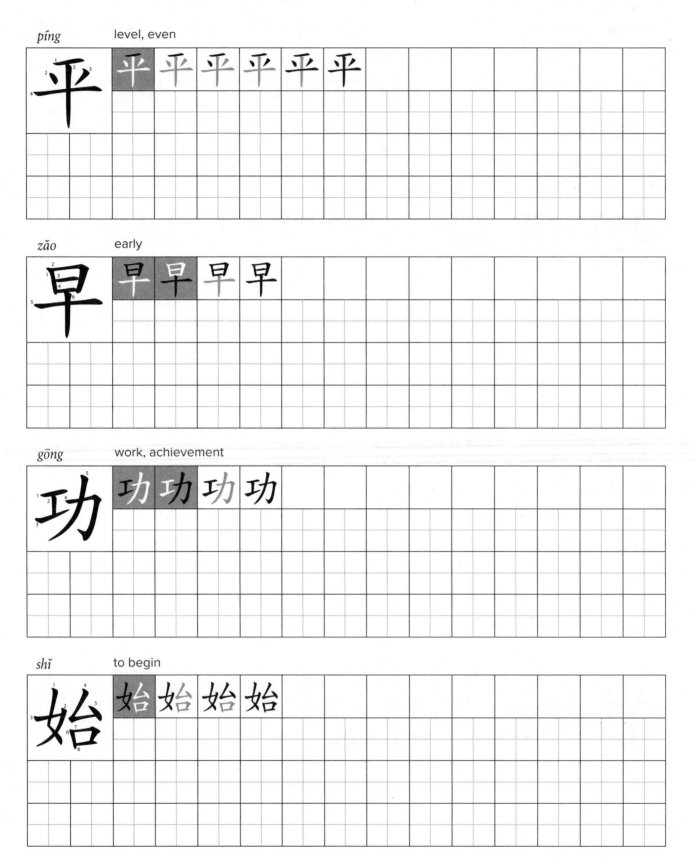

píng   level, even

平

zǎo   early

早

gōng   work, achievement

功

shǐ   to begin

始

niàn   to read aloud

念   念 念 念

lù   to record

錄 录   錄 錄 錄 錄 錄 錄 錄
     录 录 录 录 录 录 录

shuài   handsome

帥 帅   帥 帥 帥
     帅 帅 帅 帅

kù   cool

酷   酷 酷 酷 酷 酷 酷 酷 酷 酷 酷 酷 酷

Lesson 8: School Life

Diary Entry: A Typical School Day

piān   (measure word for essays, articles, etc.)

篇 | 篇 篇 篇 篇 篇 篇 篇 篇 篇 篇

jì   record

記 记 | 记 记 记 / 记 记 记

lèi   tired

累 | 累 累 累 累 累

chuáng   bed

床 | 床 床 床 床

xǐ　　to wash

洗　　洗 洗 洗

zǎo　　bath

澡　　澡 澡 澡 澡 澡 澡

biān　　side

邊 边　　邊 邊 邊 邊 邊
　　　　边 边 边

fā　　to emit, to issue

發 发　　發 發 發 發 發 發 發
　　　　发 发 发 发 发 发

xīn   new

新 新 新 新 新

nǎo   brain

腦 脑 腦 腦 腦 腦 腦 腦 腦 腦 腦 腦
脑 脑 脑 脑 脑 脑

cān   meal

餐 餐 餐 餐 餐 餐 餐

tīng   hall

廳 厅 廳 廳 廳
厅 厅 厅

wǎng　　　net

網　网　網 網 網 網 網 網 網
　　　　网 网 网 网 网 网

sù　　　to lodge for the night

宿　宿 宿 宿 宿 宿

shè　　　house

舍　舍 舍 舍 舍 舍 舍

zhèng　　　just, upright

正　正 正 正 正 正 正 正

qián front, before

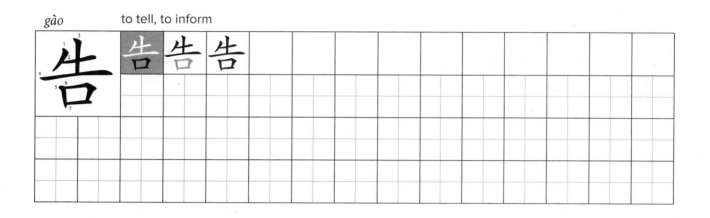

gào to tell, to inform

sù to tell, to sue

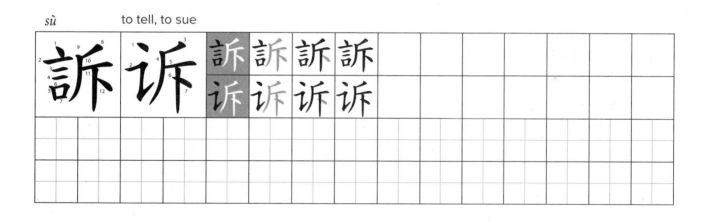

yǐ already

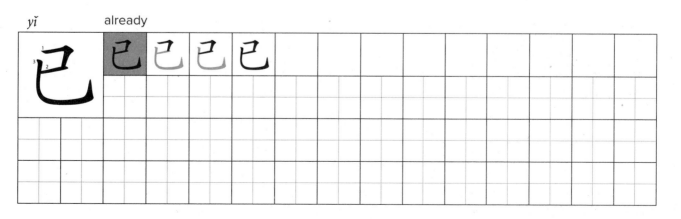

jīng   to pass through

經 经 經 經 經 經 經
経 经 经 经 经 经

zhī   to know

知 知 知 知 知

dào   path, way

道 道 道 道 道 道 道

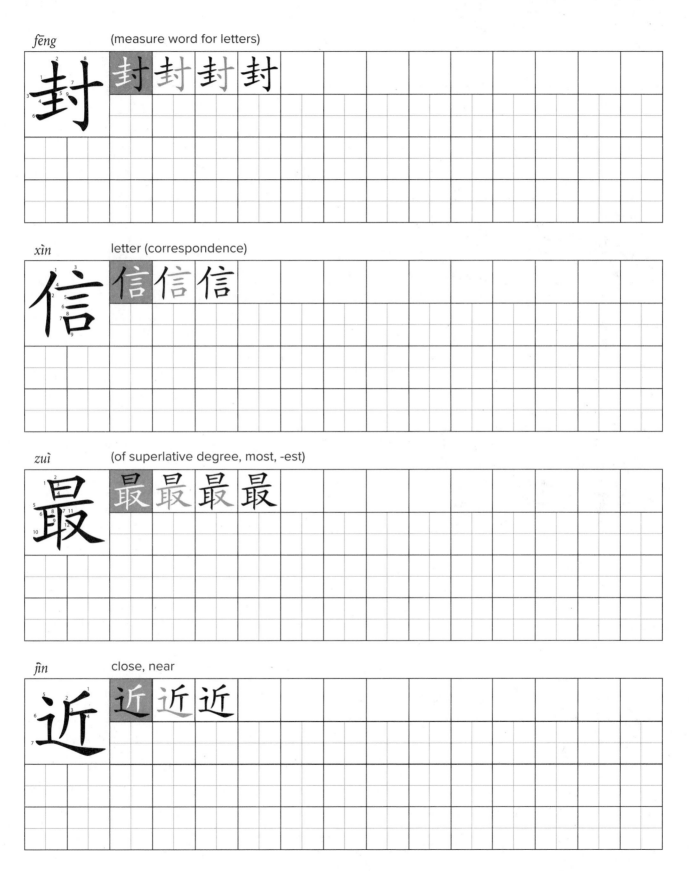

fēng　(measure word for letters)

xìn　letter (correspondence)

zuì　(of superlative degree, most, -est)

jìn　close, near

chú   apart from

除 除 除 除 除 除 除

除 除 除 除 除

zhuān   special

專 专 專 專 專 專 專 專

专 专 专 专

yè   occupation, profession

業 业 業 業 業 業 業 業 業

业 业

xī   to hope; hope

希 希 希 希 希

wàng   to hope, to expect

望 望 望 望 望 望

néng   can, to be able to

能 能 能 能 能 能 能

yòng   to use

用 用 用 用 用 用

xiào   to laugh at, to laugh, to smile

笑 笑 笑 笑 笑

zhù　to wish (well)

祝　祝 祝 祝 祝

Lesson 9: Shopping

Dialogue 1: Shopping for Clothes

shāng commerce, business

商　商 商 商 商 商 商 商 商 商 商

diàn store, shop

店　店 店 店 店 店 店 店

mǎi to buy

買 买　買 買 買 買
买 买 买 买 买 买

dōng (component of 東西 /东西: things, objects); east

東 东　東 東 東 東 東
东 东 东 东

xī   (component of 東西 /东西: things; objects); west

西　西　西

shòu   sale; to sell

售　售　售　售

huò   merchandise

貨　货　货　货　货　货
　　　　货　货　货　货

yuán   member, personnel

員　员　員　員　員　員
　　　　员　员　员　员

fú   clothing

服

服服服

jiàn   (measure word for shirts, jackets, coats, etc.)

件

件件件件件

chèn   lining

襯衬

襯襯襯襯
衬衬衬

shān   shirt

衫

衫衫衫衫

yán face, countenance

颜 颜 颜 颜 颜 颜 颜
颜 颜 颜 颜 颜

sè color

色 色 色 色 色
色

huáng yellow

黄 黄 黄 黄 黄 黄 黄 黄
黄 黄 黄 黄 黄 黄 黄 黄 黄

hóng red

红 红 红 红
红 红 红

chuān　to wear, to put on

穿　穿 穿

tiáo　(measure word for pants and long, thin objects)

條 条　條 條 條 條 條
　　　条 条 条 条 条

kù　pants

褲 褲　褲 褲 褲 褲 褲 褲
　　　褲 褲 褲 褲 褲 褲

yí　suitable, appropriate

宜　宜 宜 宜

rú　　　as, if

如　如 如 如

guǒ　　　fruit, result

果　果 果 果

cháng　　　long

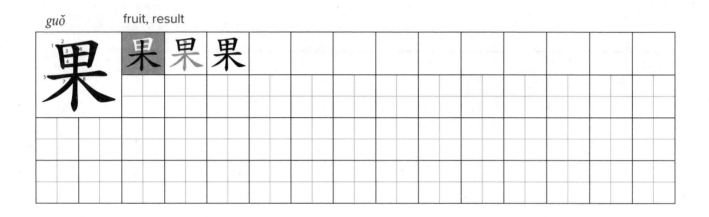

長 长　長 長 長 長 長 長 長 長 長
　　　长 长 长 长 长 长

duǎn　　　short

短　短 短 短 短 短 短 短

hé to suit, to fit

合 合 合 合 合 合

shì to suit, to be appropriate

適 适 适 适 适 适 适
适 适 适 适

gòng altogether

共 共 共 共 共

shǎo few, little, less

少 少 少 少

qián　　　money

錢　钱

kuài　　　(measure word for the basic Chinese monetary unit)

塊　块

máo　　　(measure word for 1/10 of a kuai, dime [in US money])

毛

fēn　　　(measure word for 1/100 of a kuai, cent [in US money])

分

bǎi   hundred

百　百　百　百　百

shuāng (measure word for a pair)

雙 双 雙 雙 雙 雙 雙
双 双 双

xié shoes

鞋 鞋 鞋 鞋 鞋 鞋 鞋

huàn to exchange, to change

換 換 換 換 換 換 換 換
換 換 換 換 換

hēi black

黑 黑 黑 黑

suī　　　although

雖 虽　　雖 雖 雖 雖 雖 雖 雖
　　　　虫 虫 虫 虫 虫 虫 虫

rán　　　right, correct, like that

然　　然 然 然 然 然 然 然

zhǒng　　　(measure word for kinds, sorts, types)

種 种　　種 種 種 種 種 種 種 種 種
　　　　种 种 种 种 种

tǐng　　　very, rather

挺　　挺 挺 挺 挺 挺 挺 挺

tā   it

它 它 它 它

shuā   to brush, to swipe

刷 刷 刷 刷 刷 刷 刷

kǎ   card

卡 卡 卡 卡 卡 卡 卡 卡

shōu   to receive, to accept

收 收 收 收 收

guò   to pass

過 过 過過過過過過
过过过

付   to pay

fù   to pay

付付付

Lesson 10: Transportation

Dialogue: Going Home for Winter Vacation

hán   cold

寒 　寒寒寒寒寒寒寒寒

jià   vacation

假 　假假假假假假假假

fēi   to fly

飛 飞 飛飛飛飛飛飛飛
　　 飞飞飞

jī   machine

機 机 機機機機
　　 机机机

piào ticket

票 票票票票

chǎng field

場场 場場場場場
        场场场场场

qì steam, gas

汽 汽汽汽

chē vehicle, car

車车 車車
     车车

huò　or

或

或 或 或 或 或

zhě　(component of 或者: or)

者

者 者 者 者 者

dì　ground; (particle)

地

地 地 地

tiě　iron

鐵 铁

鐵 鐵 鐵 鐵 鐵
铁 铁 铁 铁

zhàn　　　(measure word for bus stops, train stops, etc.)

站　站 站 站

lù　　　green

綠 绿　绿 绿 绿
　　　绿 绿 绿

xiàn　　　line, route

線 线　線 線 線 線
　　　线 线 线

lán　　　blue

藍 蓝　藍 藍 藍 藍 藍 藍 藍 藍 藍 藍 藍
　　　　藍
　　　蓝 蓝 蓝 蓝 蓝 蓝 蓝 蓝 蓝

má   hemp

麻 | 麻 | 麻 | 麻 | 麻 | 麻

fán   to bother, to trouble

煩 | 烦 | 煩烦 | 烦烦 | 烦烦

chū   to go out

出 | 出 | 出 | 出 | 出 | 出

zū   to rent

租 | 租 | 租 | 租

sòng   to see off or out, to take (someone somewhere)

送　送 送 送 送 送

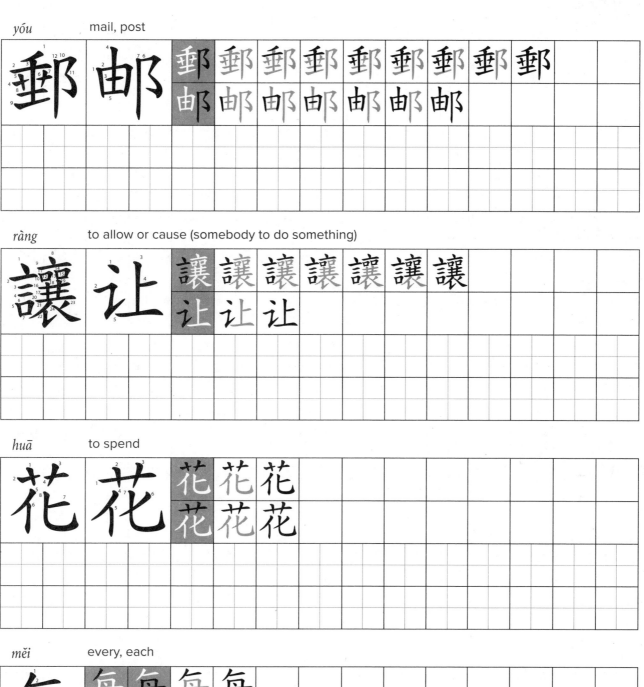

yóu   mail, post

郵 邮

ràng   to allow or cause (somebody to do something)

讓 让

huā   to spend

花 花

měi   every, each

每

chéng   town

城 城 城 城 城 城 城 城 城

shì   city

市 市 市 市 市

tè   special

特 特 特 特 特 特 特 特

sù   speed

速 速 速 速 速 速 速 速

jǐn   tense, tight

緊

zì   self

自

jǐ   self

己

INDEX A
Characters by Pinyin

P = *Pinyin*, **T** = Traditional form, **S** = Simplified form, **L** = Lesson, **B** = Basics

*Some simplified and traditional characters that appear identical are technically considered to have a different number of strokes. Where this is the case, we present the stroke orders for both the simplified and traditional versions of the character to highlight this difference.

P	T	S	Definition	L	Page
fēi	啡		(component of 咖啡: coffee)	5	63
fēn	分		(measure word for 1/100 of a kuai, cent)	9	102
fēng	封		(measure word for letters)	8	91
fú	服		clothing	9	97
fù	復	复	to repeat, to duplicate	7	77
fù	付		to pay	9	107
gāo	高		(a family name), tall, high	2	31
gào	告		to tell, to inform	8	89
gē	戈		dagger-axe	B	5
gē	哥		older brother	2	30
gē	歌		song	4	51
gè/ge	個	个	(measure word for many common, everyday objects)	2	28
gěi	給	给	to give	5	64
gēn	跟		with	6	76
gōng	工		labor, work	B	4
gōng	弓		bow	B	4
gōng	公		public	6	72
gōng	功		work, achievement	7	82
gòng	共		altogether	9	101
guǎn	館	馆	place or building (for a service, social, or cultural use)	5	65
guì	貴	贵	honorable, expensive	1	18
guó	國	国	country, nation	1	25
guǒ	果		fruit, result	9	100
guò	過	过	to pass	9	107
hái	孩		child	2	29
hái	還	还	still, additionally, alternatively	3	41
hán	寒		cold	10	109
hàn	漢	汉	Chinese ethnicity	7	81
hǎo	好		fine, good, nice, OK, it's settled	1	17
hào	號	号	(measure word for position in a numerical series, day of the month)	3	37
hē	喝		to drink	5	62
hé	和		and	2	34
hé	合		to suit, to fit	9	101
hēi	黑		black	9	104
hěn	很		very	3	46
hóng	紅	红	red	9	98
hòu	候		time, season; to await	4	53
hòu	後	后	after, behind, rear	6	70
huā	花		to spend	10	115
huà	話	话	speech	6	67
huān	歡	欢	happy, joyous	3	41
huàn	換	换	to exchange, to change	9	104
huáng	黃	黄	yellow	9	98
huí	回		to return	5	66
huì	會	会	meeting	6	69
huǒ	火		fire	B	6
huò	貨	货	merchandise	9	96
huò	或		or	10	111
jī	機	机	machine	10	109
jí	級	级	level, rank	6	70
jǐ	幾	几	how many, some, a few	2	33
jǐ	己		self	10	117
jì	記	记	record	8	85
jiā	家		family, home	2	33
jià	假		vacation	10	109
jiān	間	间	during (a time period), between (two sides)	6	68
jiàn	見	见	to see	3	43
jiàn	件		(measure word for shirts, jackets, coats, etc.)	9	97
jiāo	教		to teach	7	78
jiào	叫		to be called, to call	1	19
jié	節	节	(measure word for class periods)	6	69
jiě	姐		older sister	1	19
jiè	介		to be situated between	5	60
jīn	金		gold	B	9
jīn	今		today, now	3	38

P = *Pinyin*, **T** = Traditional form, **S** = Simplified form, **L** = Lesson, **B** = Basics

P	T	S	Definition	L	Page
jǐn	緊	紧	tense, tight	10	117
jìn	進	进	to enter	5	59
jìn	近		close, near	8	91
jīng	京		capital city	1	25
jīng	經	经	to pass through	8	90
jiǔ	九		nine	B	15
jiǔ	久		long (of time)	4	56
jiù	就		precisely, exactly	6	67
jué	覺	觉	to feel, to think	4	56
kā	咖		(component of 咖啡: coffee)	5	62
kǎ	卡		card	9	106
kāi	開	开	to open, to hold (a meeting, party, etc.)	6	69
kàn	看		to watch, to look, to read	4	50
kǎo	考		to give or take a test	6	70
kě	可		but	3	41
kè	刻		quarter (of an hour)	3	45
kè	客		guest	4	54
kè	課	课	class, course, lesson	6	69
kòng	空		free time	6	71
kǒu	口		mouth	B	2
kù	酷		cool	7	83
kù	褲	裤	pants	9	99
kuài	快		fast, quick; quickly	5	59
kuài	塊	块	(measure word for the basic Chinese monetary unit)	9	102
lái	來	来	to come	5	59
lán	藍	蓝	blue	10	112
lǎo	老		old	1	23
le	了		(particle)	3	40
lèi	累		tired	8	85
lǐ	李		(a family name), plum	1	21
lǐ	裡	里	inside	7	79
lì	力		power	B	1
liàn	練	练	to drill	6	74
liǎng	兩	两	two, a couple of	2	33
liàng	亮		bright	5	61
liáo	聊		to chat	5	65
liù	六		six	B	14

P	T	S	Definition	L	Page
lù	錄	录	to record	7	83
lù	律		law, rule	2	34
lǜ	綠	绿	green	10	112
mā	媽	妈	mother, mom	2	28
má	麻		hemp	10	113
mǎ	馬	马	horse	B	10
ma	嗎	吗	(question particle)	1	23
mǎi	買	买	to buy	9	95
màn	慢		slow	7	77
máng	忙		busy	3	46
máo	毛		(measure word for 1/10 of a kuai, dime [in US money])	9	102
me	麼	么	(question particle)	1	19
méi	沒	没	not	2	31
měi	美		beautiful	1	26
měi	每		every, each	10	115
mèi	妹		younger sister	2	33
mén	門	门	door	B	9
men	們	们	(plural suffix)	3	42
mì	糸		fine silk	B	7
miàn	面		face	6	76
míng	名		name	1	20
míng	明		bright	3	46
mò	末		end	4	49
mù	木		wood	B	6
mù	目		eye	B	7
nǎ	哪	哪	where	5	61
nà	那	那	that	2	27
nán	男		male	2	29
nán	難	难	difficult	7	81
nǎo	腦	脑	brain	8	87
ne	呢		(question particle)	1	18
néng	能		can, to be able to	8	93
nǐ	你		you	1	17
nián	年		year	3	38
niàn	念		to read aloud	7	83
nín	您		you (honorific for 你)	6	67
niǔ	紐	纽	knob, button	1	26
nǚ	女		woman	B	3
péng	朋		friend	1	21
piān	篇		(measure word for articles, etc)	8	85

P = *Pinyin*, T = Traditional form, S = Simplified form, L = Lesson, B = Basics

P	T	S	Definition	L	Page
piàn	片		flat, thin piece	2	27
piào	漂		(component of 漂亮: pretty)	5	61
piào	票		ticket	10	110
píng	瓶		(measure word for bottled liquid, etc.)	5	63
píng	平		level, even	7	82
qī	七		seven	B	14
qī	期		period (of time)	3	37
qǐ	起	起	to rise	5	64
qì	氣	气	air	6	73
qì	汽		steam, gas	10	110
qián	前		front, before	8	89
qián	錢	钱	money	9	102
qǐng	請	请	please (polite form of request), to treat or to invite (somebody)	1	17
qiú	球		ball	4	49
qù	去		to go	4	54
rán	然		right, correct; like that	9	105
ràng	讓	让	to allow or cause (somebody to do something)	10	115
rén	人		person	B	1
rén	人		people, person	1	24
rèn	認	认	to recognize	3	47
rì	日		sun	B	5
róng	容		to allow, to tolerate	7	80
sān	三		three	B	13
sè	色		color	9	98
shān	衫		shirt	9	97
shāng	商		commerce, business	9	95
shàng	上		above; top	3	43
shǎo	少		few, little, less	9	101
shào	紹	绍	to carry on, to continue	5	60
shè	舍		house	8	88
shéi	誰	谁	who	2	29
shén	什		what	1	19
shēng	生		to give birth to, to be born	1	20

P	T	S	Definition	L	Page
shī	師	师	teacher	1	23
shí	食		eat	B	10
shí	十		ten	B	15
shí	識	识	to recognize	3	47
shí	時	时	time	4	53
shǐ	始		to begin	7	82
shì	示		show	B	7
shì	是		to be	1	23
shì	事		matter, affair, event	3	45
shì	視	视	vision	4	50
shì	試	试	test; to try, to experiment	6	70
shì	室		room	6	72
shì	適	适	to suit, to be appropriate	9	101
shì	市		city	10	116
shōu	收		to receive, to accept	9	106
shǒu	手		hand	B	5
shòu	售		sale; to sell	9	96
shū	書	书	book	4	52
shuā	刷		to brush, to swipe	9	106
shuài	帥	帅	handsome	7	84
shuāng	雙	双	(measure word for a pair)	9	104
shuǐ	水		water	B	6
shuì	睡		to sleep	4	58
shuō	說	说	to say; to speak	6	75
sī	思		to think	4	57
sì	四		four	B	13
sòng	送		to see off or out; to take (someone somewhere)	10	114
sù	宿		to lodge for the night	8	88
sù	訴	诉	to tell, to sue	8	89
sù	速		speed	10	116
suàn	算		to calculate	4	58
suī	雖	虽	although	9	105
suì	歲	岁	year (of age)	3	38
suǒ	所		place; (component of 所以: therefore, so)	4	55
tā	她		she, her	2	29
tā	他		he, him	2	30

P = *Pinyin*, **T** = Traditional form, **S** = Simplified form, **L** = Lesson, **B** = Basics

P = Pinyin, **T** = Traditional form, **S** = Simplified form, **L** = Lesson, **B** = Basics

P	T	S	Definition	L	Page
yǐ	以		with	4	55
yì	意		meaning	4	57
yì	易		easy	7	81
yīn	因		cause, reason; because	3	47
yīn	音		sound	4	52
yīng	英	英	flower, hero; Britain	2	35
yǐng	影		shadow	4	53
yòng	用		to use	8	93
yóu	郵	邮	mail, post	10	115
yǒu	友		friend	1	21
yǒu	有		to have, to exist	2	31
yòu	又		right hand, again	B	1
yǔ	雨		rain	B	10
yǔ	語	语	language	7	80
yù	預	预	in advance, beforehand	7	79
yuán	員	员	member, personnel	9	96
yuē	約	约	agreement, appointment	1	26
yuè	月		moon	B	6
yuè	樂	乐	music	4	52
zài	再		again	3	43
zài	在		to be present; at (a place)	3	45
zǎo	早		early	7	82
zǎo	澡		bath	8	86
zěn	怎		how	3	39
zhàn	站		(measure words for bus stops, train stops, etc.)	10	112
zhāng	張	张	(measure word for flat objects such as paper, pictures, etc.)	7	78
zhǎo	找		to look for	4	58
zhào	照		photograph, to illuminate; to shine	2	27
zhě	者		(component of 或者: or)	10	111
zhè	這	这	this	2	28
zhēn	真		true; real(ly)	7	79
zhèng	正		just, upright	8	88
zhī	枝		(measure word for long, thin, inflexible objects such as pens, pencils, etc.)	7	77
zhī	知		to know	8	90
zhǐ	只		only	4	57
zhǐ	紙	纸	paper	7	78
zhōng	中		center, middle	1	25
zhǒng	種	种	(measure word for kinds, sorts, types)	9	105
zhōu	週	周	week, cycle	4	49
zhù	祝		to wish (well)	8	94
zhuān	專	专	special	8	92
zhuī	隹		short-tailed bird	B	10
zhǔn	準	准	standard, criterion	6	74
zǐ	子		child	B	3
zì	字		character	1	20
zì	自		self	10	117
zǒu	走		walk	B	9
zū	租		to rent	10	113
zú	足		foot	B	9
zuì	最		(of superlative degree, most, -est)	8	91
zuó	昨		yesterday	4	54
zuò	作		to work, to do	2	34
zuò	做		to do	2	34
zuò	坐		to sit	5	61

P = *Pinyin*, **T** = Traditional form, **S** = Simplified form, **L** = Lesson, **B** = Basics

INDEX B
Characters by Lesson and Pinyin

P	T	S	Definition	L	Page	P	T	S	Definition	L	Page
bā	八		eight	B	14	yán	言		speech	B	8
bèi	貝	贝	cowrie shell	B	8	yāo	幺		tiny; small	B	4
cùn	寸		inch	B	3	yī	衣		clothing	B	8
dà	大		big	B	3	yī	一		one	B	13
dāo	刀		knife	B	1	yòu	又		right hand, again	B	1
ěr	耳		ear	B	8	yǔ	雨		rain	B	10
èr	二		two	B	13	yuè	月		moon	B	6
gē	戈		dagger-axe	B	5	zhuī	佳		short-tailed bird	B	10
gōng	工		labor, work	B	4	zǐ	子		child	B	3
gōng	弓		bow	B	4	zǒu	走		walk	B	9
huǒ	火		fire	B	6	zú	足		foot	B	9
jīn	金		gold	B	9	běi	北		north	1	25
jiǔ	九		nine	B	15	bù	不		not, no	1	24
kǒu	口		mouth	B	2	guì	貴	贵	honorable, expensive	1	18
lì	力		power	B	1	guó	國	国	country, nation	1	25
liù	六		six	B	14	hǎo	好		fine, good, nice, OK, it's settled	1	17
mǎ	馬	马	horse	B	10						
mén	門	门	door	B	9	jiào	叫		to be called, to call	1	19
mì	糸		fine silk	B	7	jiě	姐		older sister	1	19
mù	木		wood	B	6	jīng	京		capital city	1	25
mù	目		eye	B	7	lǎo	老		old	1	23
nǚ	女		woman	B	3	lǐ	李		(a family name), plum	1	21
qī	七		seven	B	14	ma	嗎	吗	(question particle)	1	23
rén	人		person	B	1	měi	美		beautiful	1	26
rì	日		sun	B	5	míng	名		name	1	20
sān	三		three	B	13	me	麼	么	(question particle)	1	19
shí	食		eat	B	10	ne	呢		(question particle)	1	18
shí	十		ten	B	15	nǐ	你		you	1	17
shì	示		show	B	7	niǔ	紐	纽	knob, button	1	26
shǒu	手		hand	B	5	péng	朋		friend	1	21
shuǐ	水		water	B	6	qǐng	請	请	please (polite form of request), to treat or to invite (somebody)	1	17
sì	四		four	B	13						
tián	田		field	B	7	rén	人		people, person	1	24
tǔ	土		earth	B	2	shén	什		what	1	19
wéi	囗		enclose	B	2	shēng	生		to give birth to, to be born	1	20
wǔ	五		five	B	14						
xī	夕		sunset	B	2	shī	師	师	teacher	1	23
xiǎo	小		small	B	4	shì	是		to be	1	23
xīn	心		heart	B	5						

P = *Pinyin*, T = Traditional form, S = Simplified form, L = Lesson, B = Basics

P	T	S	Definition	L	Page
wáng	王		(a family name), king	1	21
wèn	問	问	to ask (a question)	1	17
wǒ	我		I, me	1	18
xiān	先		first	1	20
xìng	姓		(one's) family name is . . . ; family name	1	18
xué	學	学	to study	1	24
yě	也		too, also	1	24
yǒu	友		friend	1	21
yuē	約	约	agreement, appointment	1	26
zhōng	中		center, middle	1	25
zì	字		character	1	20
ài	愛	爱	love; to love	2	36
bà	爸		father, dad	2	28
bái	白		(a family name), white	2	35
de	的		(a possessive or descriptive particle)	2	27
dì	弟		younger brother	2	30
dōu	都	都	both, all	2	35
ér	兒	儿	son, child	2	30
gāo	高		(a family name), tall, high	2	31
gē	哥		older brother	2	30
gè/ge	個	个	(measure word for many common everyday objects)	2	28
hái	孩		child	2	29
hé	和		and	2	34
jǐ	幾	几	how many, some, a few	2	33
jiā	家		family, home	2	33
liǎng	兩	两	two, a couple of	2	33
lù	律		law, rule	2	34
mā	媽	妈	mother, mom	2	28
méi	沒	没	not	2	31
mèi	妹		younger sister	2	33
nà	那	那	that	2	27
nán	男		male	2	29
piàn	片		flat, thin piece	2	27
shéi	誰	谁	who	2	29
tā	她		she, her	2	29
tā	他		he, him	2	30
wén	文		(written) language, script	2	31
yī	醫	医	doctor, medicine	2	35
yīng	英	英	flower, hero; Britain	2	35
yǒu	有		to have, to exist	2	31
zhào	照		photograph; to illuminate, to shine	2	27
zhè	這	这	this	2	28
zuò	作		to work, to do	2	34
zuò	做		to do	2	34
bàn	半		half, half an hour	3	42
cài	菜	菜	dish, cuisine	3	41
chī	吃		to eat	3	39
diǎn	點	点	o'clock (lit. dot, point, thus "points on the clock")	3	42
duō	多		how many/much, to what extent	3	38
fàn	飯	饭	meal, (cooked) rice	3	39
hái	還	还	still, additionally; alternatively	3	41
hào	號	号	(measure word for position in a numerical series, day of the month)	3	37
hěn	很		very	3	46
huān	歡	欢	happy, joyous	3	41
jiàn	見	见	to see	3	43
jīn	今		today, now	3	38
kě	可		but	3	41
kè	刻		quarter (of an hour)	3	45
le	了		(particle)	3	40
máng	忙		busy	3	46
men	們	们	(plural suffix)	3	42
míng	明		bright	3	46
nián	年		year	3	38
qī	期		period (of time)	3	37
rèn	認	认	to recognize	3	47
shàng	上		above; top	3	43
shí	識	识	to recognize	3	47
shì	事		matter, affair, event	3	45
suì	歲	岁	year (of age)	3	38

P = *Pinyin,* **T** = Traditional form, **S** = Simplified form, **L** = Lesson, **B** = Basics

P	T	S	Definition	L	Page
tài	太		too, extremely	3	40
tiān	天		day	3	37
tóng	同		same	3	47
wǎn	晚	晚	evening; late	3	42
wèi	為	为	for	3	46
xǐ	喜		to like; happy	3	40
xiàn	現	现	now	3	45
xiè	謝	谢	to thank	3	40
xīng	星		star	3	37
yàng	樣	样	shape, appearance, manner	3	39
yīn	因		cause, reason; because	3	47
zài	再		again	3	43
zài	在		to be present; at (a place)	3	45
zěn	怎		how	3	39
bié	別	别	other	4	58
cháng	常		often	4	53
chàng	唱		to sing	4	50
cuò	錯	错	wrong	4	56
dǎ	打		to hit	4	49
de	得		(particle)	4	57
diàn	電	电	electricity	4	50
duì	對	对	right, correct	4	52
gē	歌		song	4	51
hòu	候		time, season; to await	4	53
jiǔ	久		long (of time)	4	56
jué	覺	觉	to feel, to think	4	56
kàn	看		to watch, to look, to read	4	50
kè	客		guest	4	54
mò	末		end	4	49
qiú	球		ball	4	49
qù	去		to go	4	54
shí	時	时	time	4	53
shì	視	视	vision	4	50
shū	書	书	book	4	52
shuì	睡	睡	to sleep	4	58
sī	思		to think	4	57
suàn	算		to calculate	4	58
suǒ	所		place; (component of 所以: therefore, so)	4	55
tiào	跳		to jump	4	51
tīng	聽	听	to listen	4	51
wài	外		outside	4	54
wǔ	舞		to dance; dance	4	51
xiǎng	想		to want to, would like to	4	56
yǐ	以		with	4	55
yì	意		meaning	4	57
yīn	音		sound	4	52
yǐng	影		shadow	4	53
yuè	樂	乐	music	4	52
zhǎo	找		to look for	4	58
zhǐ	只		only	4	57
zhōu	週	周	week, cycle	4	49
zuó	昨		yesterday	4	54
ba	吧		(a sentence-final particle)	5	63
bēi	杯		(measure word for things contained in a cup or glass)	5	64
cái	才		not until, only then	5	66
chá	茶	茶	tea	5	62
fēi	啡		(component of 咖啡: coffee)	5	63
gěi	給	给	to give	5	64
guǎn	館	馆	place or building (for a service, social, or cultural use)	5	65
hē	喝		to drink	5	62
huí	回		to return	5	66
jiè	介		to be situated between	5	60
jìn	進	进	to enter	5	59
kā	咖		(component of 咖啡: coffee)	5	62
kuài	快		fast, quick; quickly	5	59
lái	來	来	to come	5	59
liàng	亮	亮	bright	5	61
liáo	聊		to chat	5	65
nǎ	哪	哪	where	5	61
piào	漂		(component of 漂亮: pretty)	5	61

P = *Pinyin*, **T** = Traditional form, **S** = Simplified form, **L** = Lesson, **B** = Basics

P	T	S	Definition	L	Page
píng	瓶		(measure word for bottled liquid, etc.)	5	63
qǐ	起	起	to rise	5	64
shào	紹	绍	to carry on, to continue	5	60
tú	圖	图	picture, chart, drawing	5	65
wán	玩		to have fun, to play	5	65
xià	下		below, under	5	60
xiào	校		school	5	62
xìng	興	兴	mood, interest	5	60
ya	呀		(interjectory particle used to soften a question)	5	59
yào	要		to want	5	63
zuò	坐		to sit	5	61
a	啊	啊	(a sentence-final particle of exclamation, interrogation, etc.)	6	75
bàn	辦	办	to manage	6	72
bāng	幫	帮	to help	6	74
bèi	備	备	to prepare	6	74
biàn	便		convenient, handy	6	71
dàn	但		but	6	75
dào	到		to go to, to arrive	6	71
děng	等		to wait, to wait for	6	73
fāng	方		square, method	6	71
gēn	跟		with	6	76
gōng	公		public	6	72
hòu	後	后	after, behind, rear	6	71
huà	話	话	speech	6	67
huì	會	会	meeting	6	69
jí	級	级	level, rank	6	70
jiān	間	间	during (a time period), between (two sides)	6	68
jié	節	节	(measure word for class periods)	6	69
jiù	就		precisely, exactly	6	67
kāi	開	开	to open, to hold (a meeting, party, etc.)	6	69
kǎo	考		to give or take a test	6	70
kè	課	课	class, course, lesson	6	69
kòng	空		free time	6	71
liàn	練	练	to drill	6	74
miàn	面		face	6	76
nín	您		you (honorific for 你)	6	67
qì	氣	气	air	6	73
shì	室		room	6	72
shì	試	试	test; to try, to experiment	6	70
shuō	說	说	to say, to speak	6	75
tí	題	题	topic, question	6	68
wéi/wèi	喂		(on telephone) Hello!, Hey!	6	67
wèi	位		(polite measure word for people)	6	68
wǔ	午		noon	6	68
xí	習	习	to practice	6	75
xíng	行		all right, OK	6	72
zhǔn	準	准	standard, criterion	6	74
bǐ	筆	笔	pen	7	78
cí	詞	词	word	7	81
dì	第		(prefix for ordinal numbers)	7	80
dǒng	懂	懂	to understand	7	79
fǎ	法		law, rule, method	7	80
fù	復	复	to repeat, to duplicate	7	77
gōng	功		work, achievement	7	82
hàn	漢	汉	Chinese ethnicity	7	81
jiāo	教		to teach	7	78
kù	酷		cool	7	83
lǐ	裡	里	inside	7	79
lù	錄	录	to record	7	83
màn	慢		slow	7	77
nán	難	难	difficult	7	81
niàn	念		to read aloud	7	83
píng	平		level, even	7	82
róng	容		to allow, to tolerate	7	80
shǐ	始		to begin	7	82
shuài	帥	帅	handsome	7	84
xiě	寫	写	to write	7	77
yì	易		easy	7	81

P = Pinyin, **T** = Traditional form, **S** = Simplified form, **L** = Lesson, **B** = Basics

P = *Pinyin*, T = Traditional form, S = Simplified form, L = Lesson, B = Basics

P	T	S	Definition	L	Page	P	T	S	Definition	L	Page
mǎi	買	买	to buy	9	95	chū	出		to go out	10	113
máo	毛		(measure word for 1/10 of a kuai, dime [in US money])	9	102	dì	地		ground; (particle)	10	111
						fán	煩	烦	to bother, to trouble	10	113
qián	錢	钱	money	9	102	fēi	飛	飞	to fly	10	109
rán	然		right, correct; like that	9	105	hán	寒		cold	10	109
sè	色		color	9	98	huā	花	花	to spend	10	115
shān	衫		shirt	9	97	huò	或		or	10	111
shāng	商		commerce, business	9	95	jī	機	机	machine	10	109
shǎo	少		few, little, less	9	101	jǐ	己		self	10	117
shì	適	适	to suit, to be appropriate	9	101	jiǎ	假		vacation	10	109
						jǐn	緊	紧	tense, tight	10	117
shōu	收		to receive, to accept	9	106	lán	藍	蓝	blue	10	112
shòu	售		sale; to sell	9	96	lǜ	綠	绿	green	10	112
shuā	刷		to brush, to swipe	9	106	má	麻		hemp	10	113
shuāng	雙	双	(measure word for a pair)	9	104	měi	每		every, each	10	115
						piào	票		ticket	10	110
suī	雖	虽	although	9	105	qì	汽		steam, gas	10	110
tā	它		it	9	106	ràng	讓	让	to allow or cause (somebody to do something)	10	115
tiáo	條	条	(measure word for pants and long, thin objects)	9	99	shì	市		city	10	118
tǐng	挺		very, rather	9	105	sòng	送		to see off or out, to take (someone somewhere)	10	114
xī	西		(component of 東西 /东西: things, objects); west	9	96	sù	速		speed	10	118
						tè	特		special	10	116
						tiě	鐵	铁	iron	10	111
xié	鞋		shoes	9	104	xiàn	線	线	line	10	112
yán	顏	颜	face, countenance	9	98	yóu	郵	邮	mail, post	10	115
yí	宜		suitable, appropriate	9	99	zhàn	站		(measure words for bus stops, train stops, etc.)	10	112
yuán	員	员	member, personnel	9	96						
zhǒng	種	种	(measure word for kinds, sorts, types)	9	105	zhě	者		(component of 或者: or)	10	111
chǎng	場	场	field	10	110	zì	自		self	10	117
chē	車	车	vehicle, car	10	110	zū	租		to rent	10	113
chéng	城		town	10	116						

P = *Pinyin*, **T** = Traditional form, **S** = Simplified form, **L** = Lesson, **B** = Basics